AF480661

Barry "Superhostess" Brown

My Ridgewood Farm Experiences

BARRY "SUPERHOSTESS" BROWN

MY RIDGEWOOD FARM EXPERIENCES
by Barry Brown

ISBN 979-8-9901820-1-1 hardcover

979-8-9901820-2-8 softcover

979-8-9901820-3-5 Ebook

Cover/interior book design Barry Brown

Cover art Barry Brown

Orso Marrone Publishing
1 Ridgewood Lane
Searcy, AR 72143

Preface and Special Thanks

Welcome to the "My Experiences" series! It all began with the book in your hands, *My Ridgewood Farm Experiences*. And it began because guests at the farmhouse on Ridgewood Farm regularly asked about the history of the place.

Names of people have been changed to protect identities, as far as you know. Nearly everything in this book falls into the category of "things I heard from other people," so if anything seems offensive or slanderous, my sources are to blame not me, says I.

A large and genuine thanks to Gary Rodgers, Kim Vernon, Lydia Clark, Naomi Sechrest, and Tony Franklin, all of whom contributed to reducing and rewording the less understandable portions of my style.

The Soul of a Place

Wintery day at Ridgewood Farm. Photographer unknown, but we're pretty sure it was a caveman.

If you haven't breathed in the soul of a place, it might be because you haven't slowed down enough. Places are not very fast, generally. And to feel them, you have to sit still.

Ridgewood Farm is a beautiful place. It is a place with an old, happy soul. It has connections and relationships. It whispers if you listen closely enough. And it smiles if you slow down enough to feel it.

Morning sunbeams. Photo by Barry Brown.

So, find a place to sit. Slow down and breathe deeply. Smile and close your eyes. You'll have to open them again, and I'm not sure how you'll know to do that unless you're listening to this on audiobook. Otherwise, I'll hope you decide to come back and read on in a few minutes. Or someone nudges you awake if you get to snoring. And I'll tell you some tales about Ridgewood Farm.

Frank

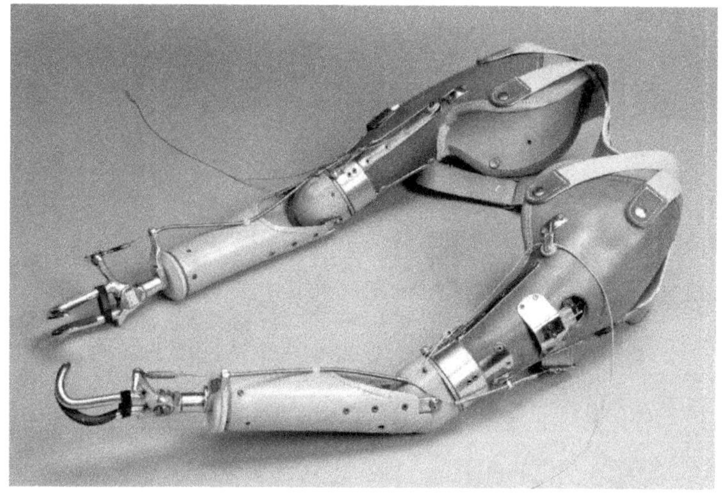

Original Photo courtesy of the Science Museum Group. Artistic alterations by Barry Brown.

My dad's boss was a one-armed man. We'll call him Frank for the purposes of this story. Where Frank's other arm would normally have been, he sported an artificial arm with a hook he opened and closed by shuffling his shoulder up and down. I remember thinking his arm and hook were more scary than cool as a kid. I reacted this way because Frank tried to endear himself to kids by grabbing a hookful of ear. The hook had no nerves in it, so he had no way to gauge how hard he grabbed. And the hook grabbed hard.

Other than the ear-grabbing, the thing was great. He used it as a letter opener, holding the envelope with his good hand and slashing the flap with the hook. When the company Christmas party was at a seafood buffet, we loved watching him crack crab legs with it.

Frank was a generous, caring man. He regularly arranged holiday parties for those who worked for him and their families. He loved holding a bingo game and passing out prizes. I still remember when you'd hit the time in the game he wanted to make it exciting. He'd yell, "Four co-ners!" at the beginning of a round. We got to put a bean on each of the four corners of our cards before he drew anything. That was like Christmas to us little kids. We felt so special. It didn't quite dawn on us that everyone else got the same advantage.

I almost killed Frank one summer. In my teens, I had a summer job working in the warehouse of Frank's electrical, industrial, and HVAC supply store. The warehouse was not climate-controlled. In the summer in Arkansas, that meant it was a prelude to hell.

One day, I was building some new shelving in the dark back part of the warehouse. My clothes stuck to my skin and I looked like someone dumped a bucket of water on me. I struggled to fill my lungs with the wet-blanket-dense, lung-scorching air.

All of a sudden, something touched the back of my neck. I spun around—still holding the hammer I was using—and nearly clocked Frank. I was swinging like Babe Ruth for the fences. Frank had held his hook in the freezer a while and then snuck up and stuck it on the back of my neck. The look on his face said he probably wouldn't do that again, and he didn't.

I don't know how Frank lost his arm. I only have my parents' stories, which is my sole way of knowing lots of stuff. My parents said when Frank was an electrical engineering student, he was in a manufacturing plant whonking around on something in a big electrical panel. Someone across the plant saw a power switch in the OFF position and thought it needed to be ON. So they threw the lever. POW! Elevendy-zillion volts zipped to the panel Frank was beating around in with a wrench and arced from the panel to the wrench and into Frank's arm. It was so badly burned it had to be removed to about the middle of his biceps.

Now, that's a horrible thing to happen, I'll give you. But that doesn't mean once it *has* happened and lots of time has gone by, the situation isn't subject to jesting and merry-making. We often sat around the break area joking about what attachments might be available in place of the hook. There was no end of pirate jokes at the workplace.

The other fellas related a tale of a fishing trip they took with Frank. They said he caught a whopper of a catfish. If you've never caught a catfish, let me tell you. They don't prefer being caught, all things being equal. They get obnoxious. One of their little tricks is to clamp down on the fishhook once you've reeled them in, rendering it nearly impossible to get them unhooked. Well, Frank was allegedly holding the catfish's mouth with his hook and the fish clamped down. He couldn't get his good hand in to remove the fishhook. He got angry and was flailing around, slinging the fish this way and that. And that's when his arm came unstrapped.

I may have forgotten to tell you he had his shirt off.

There goes the arm, still holding the catfish clamping his arm and hook, and the fishhook still connected to the fish's mouth. Out goes the line. Fortunately, the fellas had the presence of mind to grab his pole before it followed the convoy into the lake. They reeled in the catfish, still holding Frank's hook and arm in its mouth.

You might be wondering what my dad's boss Frank had to do with Ridgewood Farm. And I'll give it to you: so far, the connection feels weak at best. But hang on. I'm not done yet.

The Rat Story

Original image generated by ChatGPT, artistically reworked by Barry Brown.

The summer before I went into sixth grade, Dad came home with rats. That's an odd sentence, but it could be better. Our street was on a hill, and we lived lower than the street entrance. I could have said, "One summer, Dad came down with rats."

Like it was an illness or something. Either sentence is odd, but it was an equally odd event. One minute we didn't have any rats, and then there he was with these two rats with black and white patches.

Dad told us the backstory of these rats, which is another series of odd events. So apparently, a farmer died in a chicken house fire. His wife was pretty sure he expired specifically due to poisonous fumes put off by the burning insulation, especially after her attorney said that was a prime suable possibility.

They were building their case and must have needed some actual proof. They needed to recreate the fire event and see if the burning insulation put off poisonous fumes.

One of the interesting traits about my dad's boss Frank, aside from the missing arm, was his inclination to get his nose into things. Didn't matter if it pertained to him in any way. Well, he somehow got involved in the chicken house fire re-creation project. I have no idea how or why. He had nothing to do with chickens, chicken houses, insulation, or fires. But fortunately for me, as it turns out, he got involved and drug Dad along to the tiny chicken house test fire.

How does that turn into Dad bringing home rats? Now, that's a great question. The way the experts decided to determine whether the burning insulation put off poisonous fumes was to put lab rats in the burning mini-chicken-house and then autopsy them to see if they burnt up or died of breathing poisonous fumes. Sucks to be a lab rat if you didn't already know that. It's not always eating Cheetos your whole life and then answering questions about whether you feel overweight or depressed, like you might think.

So, Dad told us these two rats he came home with got sick before the big burn. How do you tell a rat is too sick to get burned or alternately poisoned to death? He didn't say. But he asked what would happen to those rats and the lab goobers said they would just kill them, presumably in some normal rat-killing fashion that didn't involve fire and poison gas. Dad asked if he could have them. They said yes. Probably figured he wanted to test a fire or some poison back home.

The sick scientists told Dad this breed were called hooded rats because they had that little neck scruff skin like a cat. And like a cat, you could pick them up by it and they'd go motionless.

As what we all hope is a brief aside, my farm experiences have taught me that mice, wild rats, and possums are also equipped with the Vulcan neck pinch feature.

On a few occasions, I have darted around, dodging this way and that, holding sticks, little boxes, hats, and nets, trying to trap one of the aforementioned rodents. Or "marsupials" if you ascribe to that notion about the possums.

And many times, I've eventually given up and snatched ahold of the neck scruff and walked out holding the offending critter. Frozen. Front legs T-rexing it, back legs dangling. To the utter flabbergastation or flabbergastment of the witnesses and photographers.

Back to the story. Dad showed up with these two rats. Two boy rats. Unmistakably, as you would know if you'd

Me chilling with a possum held by his/her paralyzing neck scruff. Photo by Lori Davis.

ever seen boy rats. This was the first time Dad ever mentioned the fact that he had pet rats at some point in life. I'm not sure what situation that kind of story comes up in, but we'd never heard that before.

My brother and I got super creative with the naming process, landing on Willy and Wally. I still remember, Willy was more white with black patches, and Wally was more black with white patches. They had no racial disputes as far as we could determine.

You may think to yourself, that's nasty. Rats are gross and dirty. Well, they aren't, oddly enough. They spend an inordinate amount of time cleaning and preening like cats—although they likely would be offended at the comparison. Their poop was immeasurably less gross than cats. Just little dry black tic tacs.

Willy and Wally were incredibly smart. We would take them out in the yard to play. They would run out and find a piece of dog food we threw to them. They would come back when we called their names. So smart, as a matter of fact, I decided to take them to school to show my classmates.

Willy and Wally were a big hit. At least to the students gathered around the desk looking at them. I sort of recall a number of students being a bit elsewhere while Willy and Wally were out running around. They peed on Matt's desk for entertainment. And we were entertained.

I told the rat story for decades to any and all hearers. No one ever shared any connection to the event. Not one person had the slightest knowledge of the entire weird situation. Until I met Dan.

Dan

Photo courtesy JT Hotshotting, BC, Canada. Photo edits by Barry Brown.

When I told you about Frank, I promised I'd let you know what he had to do with Ridgewood Farm. I guess I have to do the same thing with the rats. I'm starting to get behind on my promises. But Dan is critical to tying up these loose ends, so let's get started.

I was at a time in life when I chose to earn exactly what I needed to cover my meager bills. This permitted me to work infrequently, which did not resonate with most employers. But it worked just fine for the things I was doing.

I was driving professionally. Not like Jason Statham as a transporter, Clint Eastwood as a trucker, or Mario Andretti as a racecar driver. I was doing hotshot driving. Commercial hauls using a pickup truck.

I picked up RV trailers in Elkhart, Indiana for delivery all over the eastern half of the United States. I carried Sea Ark and Ranger boats from the factories to dealerships. Calico horse and livestock trailers from the thriving metropolis of Quitman, Arkansas to dealers from Texas to Alabama.

And that's how I met Dan. A friend recommended I visit Dan to see if he needed hauling done. I went by his place of business a few times without finding him there. But I'm so glad I kept trying. What an interesting friend he became!

Dan rented equipment to the film industry. Star trailers, generators, lighting, restroom trailers, make-up trailers. I think in other industries you call his facilities and grounds a "campus." That's a nicer term than "junkyard," which is more what the place reminded me of. The sort of junkyard a guy can lose himself in.

Dan's campus had been in his family forever. It had been a lumberyard since the early 1900s. The largest building was one of those old drive-thru lumber storage buildings where the wood was stacked in racks on either side. When I met Dan, it still had ancient bins of nails and screws, scabby add-on wings with shelves and wood racks, and the dust of dinosaurs everywhere.

He had a gorgeous wood-grain Chris-Craft ski boat from 1967 awaiting repairs. Also, a sailboat awaiting repairs on a trailer awaiting repairs. There was a box truck awaiting—you know, I think I'm going to cut this "awaiting repairs" list short. I only have so much room if this is going to be a single volume book, and I still have to tie this in to Ridgewood Farm.

I think whenever Dan couldn't find a tool, he just bought a new one. And judging from that main building, he almost never could find a tool. Soon after I met him, I began doing odd jobs there on the campus when I was bored between driving trips. I decided to organize the tools.

There were enough tools and replacement tools and toolboxes, I was able to put together—I swear I'm not making this up—FIVE entire toolboxes with complete sets of screwdrivers, pliers, all sizes of sockets and wrenches—English and metric, hammers, and adjustable wrenches. Tall, professional, mechanic-shop-style toolboxes. Not "granny's-kitchen-drawer" kits.

There was a room of spare trailer parts. A room for ancient electric cables and junctions for movie lighting. A room for vehicle maintenance supplies like oil, antifreeze, hitches, spare wheels and tires. There was an area with woodworking tools and the planer and tablesaw. Rooms with the detritus of a number of previous hobbies.

But that was just the big building. And probably not all of it, just what I remember. There was the office building. It contained the office itself, where Dan had his computer, a couple of couches, and enough paper piled around to represent the output of Georgia Pacific for a year or two.

The ancillary rooms connected to the office contained junk storage and accoutrements for Dan's current hobby: slot cars. Shelves of slot cars, a huge slot car track, easy chairs for sitting while racing slot cars.

Dan's place was good for puttering around. There was always some section of roof leaking that needed patching. Some portion of fence that required propping up. Some trailer that had blown a tire and needed the fender redone, or one that needed major rework due to a leaky roof.

Besides his being an all-around good guy, I enjoyed these little jobs with him because he was always full of great entertaining stories. Stories that were unlike ones I'd heard anywhere in my life. It was like Dan came from a different world than I did or something, even though we literally grew up in the same neighborhood. Like the time he was on about flying squirrels.

Rocky

Original image generated by ChatGPT, artistically reworked by Barry Brown. But this is what they look like, I swear.

Dan kept going on about the flying squirrels keeping him up all night making racket in the walls and ceiling. I thought he was batty, but we weren't at a place where I felt comfortable yet calling him out. However, he wouldn't let it go.

I had lived decades in Arkansas, romped around the woods all over, and had never seen a flying squirrel. I was sure we didn't have such a thing. So, finally, one day I said, "What are you calling flying squirrels? Just these red and gray ones running around? Are you calling them 'flying' because they jump or something?"

"No! Flying squirrels. They fly. They're squirrels. I'll bring you one next time I catch one." Sure.

Well, "sure" enough, a few days later, here he came when I was busy messing with something or other at his place, carrying a small live animal trap with an honest-to-God flying squirrel in it.

"Oh, they're called sugar gliders," you may be saying to your smart self. No, they are not. I looked it up. Dan didn't want it, so I was going to keep it as a pet for a while at least. I made a nice big wire mesh cage with hamster wheels and sticks. I had to look up what food was best and all that.

I found that sugar gliders, which look remarkably *like* flying squirrels, are marsupials. And they live somewhere. I forget where, but you can look that up if you're already out there fact-checking me. Flying squirrels are native here. I just never saw them because they only come out at night when it's too dark to see them.

My flying squirrel needed a name. I always loved the Rocky and Bulwinkle show, so Rocky it was because Bulwinkle is an unwieldy name, and he was a moose anyway. Rocky was cute as the dickens, as my family used to say, although I don't know why.

The so-called flying squirrel experts said you could keep one as a pet if you got it as a baby and trained it to be okay with people. I was never one to be hemmed in by what the experts say. Rocky was not a baby.

Rocky's house had a little nest box with soft things in it. I put a door to the outside in the house so I could get Rocky out when he was groggy and asleep. My hope was he would be less prone to go flying off in that state.

I cut the sleeve out of a sweatshirt and sewed the wrist end closed. I would put the open end up to the door in the nest box and then stir around the cage. Rocky would "escape" into the sweatshirt sleeve. I'd go sit and do my morning reading with my hand and arm down in the sleeve with him, petting and caressing him. The experts had said flying squirrels need acclimation to get accustomed to their humans.

I wouldn't say Rocky ever got accustomed to me. He never escape-escaped, like out of the house and into the sticks. But he *sort of* escaped a couple of times. I easily caught him in a live-animal trap baited with peanuts.

The first time he got away, he had lulled me into thinking we were cool. I was letting him crawl around right on me, outside the sleeve. Then all of a sudden, he jumped and popped out his hang-gliding skins. He slow-motion floated all the way to the floor. He looked like a little square squirrel pelt.

Rocky eventually made it back to the wild, released right here on Ridgewood Farm! But lest you get all excited, this is not the real tie-in. I haven't gotten Dan or Frank or the rats back to the farm yet. I am working on it. I think you need to have a better handle on Dan and his stories first.

Dan's Stories

Photo courtesy of Alamy Images. Artistically adapted by Barry Brown.

Every time I work with Dan, he has a story. Every time they are entertaining. And every time it's something I haven't heard before from any other source, despite having lived in the same community with him my whole life.

Like the time he told me about how the city water used to get treated. We get our water from the Little Red River that runs out of the dam at Greer's Ferry Lake. The water treatment facility is just outside town on the north side.

If this story was like Chevy Chase's Vegas Vacation, I'd say, "That dam water needed to be treated," or something.

Dan told me that when he was growing up, there wasn't a proper road up to the treatment facility, and the city didn't have unloading equipment up there. Any time we got a load of chemicals for treating the water, the all-call went out at the barbershops and coffee counters. Men rode horses and drove wagons. They puttered out in Model T Fords. They hand-carried the sacks of chemicals from where the delivery truck stopped to the treatment facility itself by the river.

Horses figured into a few of his stories. Another amusing one involved his

Houdini-inspired family horses. Dan recounted how several Sundays he'd be in church—First United Methodist on Main— when men would come in and tell his family their horses were out again and grazing on the courthouse lawn downtown. They'd leave the service to go round them up and take them home.

Dan's father was the mayor of Searcy for a few years. Before he was mayor, Dan's stories went, there was an annual pigeon shoot downtown. And that might sound a bit unnecessarily violent to some of you, but that would be ones of you who encounter pigeons more as park waddlers than real estate destroyers.

The brief aside in this story involves my own dad. Dad was a schoolteacher at Harding Academy, the K-12 private school associated with Harding University. The

Academy teachers were paid woefully less than Arkansas public school teachers, and at that time, Arkansas and Mississippi were always running neck-and-neck as 49th and 50th in the United States for public school teacher salary. Dad's line of work and place of employment made a summer job absolutely life or death. He repaired air conditioners all summer, and as a result, we had food.

My parents were quite religious. Religiously so, you might say. And they considered making money—even at their profession—at the expense of anything remotely looking like their church as paramount to billing God Himself directly. They saw this as worse than taboo. So whenever the church needed the air conditioning repaired, Dad did it for free. And he usually chose to volunteer me or my brother to help.

Our church had a flat roof. Whoever invented the flat roof was not as spiritually minded as my parents. In the sense that they were probably Satan-worshipers bent on the destruction of mankind. Flat roofs leak. They sag. They require the GDP of a small nation to maintain. They are unsightly, ugly, and not attractive. And they breed pigeons.

When we went on the flat roof to work on the air conditioners, inevitably, we encountered pigeon nests. Pigeons themselves. Pigeon feathers. Rotten pigeon eggs. And pigeon manure. Piles and piles of pigeon manure. All of which washed over during rains and clogged the roof drains. This created a morass of swampy pigeon filth that sat on the rooftop festering until it found some way to ooze through the flat roof and contaminate the attic spaces and stain the ceilings of the building. If pigeons could only nest in trees like normal birds.

Back to the story, now that hopefully you understand that pigeons are *NOT* winged puppies that need social justice like baby seals or something.

Every year, Dan said, the men in town would group around buildings that served as favorite pigeon roosting and pooping sites. They would bring their shotguns loaded with birdshot. The pigeons were bunched up, cooing and pooping, and emitting feathers on one building. The men at that building would go to blasting. The pigeons would take off and fly to some other building, where another group there would unload on them. And so on.

That was the annual pigeon control method for decades in Searcy, Arkansas. Then—a little-known fact, according to Dan—when his dad was mayor, he found a way that was more effective, probably safer, and more pigeon-friendly to deal with the problem. He found a sterilizing feed. The pigeons ate the feed, they became sterile, they lived happy, normal-length pigeon lives, then they expired. Leaving no new generation. There have not been pigeons pooping up the town for the forty years since. I guess the pope wouldn't condone this kind of solution—being anti-birth control, but then, the Vatican is straight-hot lousy with pigeons. More pigeons than Catholics, believe it or not.

And these Dan stories were good. They were entertaining. But they were not THE story. I mean, he had one story that was the stuff of movies. Or at least a small Netflix special or something.

The Heist

Photo courtesy of the Butler Center for Arkansas Studies, Central Arkansas Library System

Now when Dan told me this story, he didn't call it "the heist." But I thought as long as we were talking about film adaptations, that was better than "you wouldn't believe what happened to my grandparents one time. Pass me a beer."

Dan's grandparents were an interesting lot. Dan and I both tried our best to squeeze more vegetables than weeds and squash bugs out of our garden plots. This led to his stories about him helping his grandparents prepare seedlings for sale in the old days. They scattered seeds on cookie sheets covered in a thin layer of soil, and then separated them into individual plant containers when they sprouted. Hundreds. Thousands. Every year.

Which background story will tend to surprise you when I tell you they ran the Bank of Kensett. You'd have thought they ran the Feed Store of Kensett or something. Well, that's rural Arkansas. But on to our story.

Apparently, one day some fellas strode into the Bank of Kensett, located in Kensett, population 858. In Arkansas, the city limit signs tell the population, like they tell the elevation in Colorado. So, smack in the middle of The Depression, these fellas came in dressed up as bank robbers, complete with bandanas around their lower faces. They were dressed as bank robbers, incidentally, because they were bent on robbing the bank.

Dan's grandparents told the men that the safe was on a timer and only opened in the morning. Although the men had not planned ahead and packed kidnapper costumes, they improvised and took Dan's grandparents hostage.

They trundled his grandparents off to their own house and tied them up. At least their two boys, one of whom went on to be Searcy's mayor, as you learned earlier. These were not hardened, cruel robbers.

They were so not hardened, and so not cruel that they left the boys loosely tied, allowing them to get out of their bonds fairly immediately.

Dan's grandmother made breakfast and coffee in the morning as usual. Biscuits, gravy, sausage, eggs. It got to smelling so good that the robbers came out of their bandanas to have some. Then everyone went down to the bank for the grand vault opening. Their robbers did their robbing and drove off in Dan's grandparent's Model T Ford. Grand Theft Auto might want to add a thrilling variant with a Model T that tops out at about forty putt-putting miles an hour.

Dan's grandfather went to the coffee shop where the sheriff and his cronies were known to congregate and told what had happened.

If you've ever been in the rural South, you know what happened then. Everyone figured and plotted and compared which road named after which obscure tree or insect the robbers would take to exit stage left, so to speak. Each point had to be argued and reargued. It was all about elegance of argument more than getting to the point of catching the robbers, more likely than not.

The final consensus was that the robbers would have to leave the county using the only bridge going over the river at that time, and that they would likely sneak over at night. So, they gathered up a posse and moseyed over to the other side of the bridge and waited for nightfall.

Sure enough, just after dark, here came the Model T, sputtering along toward the bridge. The robbers were easily captured.

At their trial, the judge asked Dan's grandmother to identify the robbers, and she did. When asked how she could tell since they were wearing masks, she told how they removed them to eat her home-cooked breakfast.

As great a story as that is, there may be some of you a bit irritated that we seem no closer to tying this in to Ridgewood Farm than we were six chapters ago.

Getting Close

Photo and artistic adaptation by Barry Brown.

A good number of Dan's stories centered around the family business. Dan's family had owned a lumber yard.

Lumber yards were the old version of today's big box stores like Lowe's and Home Depot. They didn't have garden supplies or major home appliances. They didn't sell sodas and candy and energy drinks. They didn't sell holiday decorations or apparel. They sold lumber, of all things.

And lumber accessories. Like nails and screws. Some really stretched the boundaries and sold other building supplies like wiring and plumbing appurtenances.

Lumber stores did have little oddities that added a beauty to the world. A beauty and soul that the world is worse for no longer having. Like the wooden nickels pictured above. Like the fact that nobody got crucified over "United States" being misspelled on them. (How many of you just turned back to look and see if it was really misspelled? It was, for the rest of you.)

Wooden nickels were once everywhere. All my friends had a brown paper sack of them that we used for building little forts for plastic army men, or for targets for rubber band guns.

Brown paper sacks were once everywhere, too. They had a lot more nostalgic value than the plastic, wild-life choking, non-degradable things we use today.

In the spirit of the time, wooden nickels were an advertisement, a marketing tool. They were something to pass between a father and a son, or between boys. Now, they're a relic that sets you back $5.99 each on Ebay. Plus ten bucks for shipping.

I do remember a transitional mixed-genre store down in North Little Rock. Some kind of home center or other. They had a little area up front that sold chili dogs on paper plates, bags of chips, and cold drinks. My family often went there for supper on a Friday night and ate. Then we wandered the aisles looking at building materials to walk it off. That's the sort of family I grew up in.

Dan told me that all the local builders and tradesmen used his family's lumber yard for their supplies. But approximately zero of them had a head for business. They'd borrow money to start a house. They'd work along, buying more supplies and making payments to their laborers. Then, when all was said and done, they'd get paid for the house, pay their bill for supplies, and have nothing left or still owe a little.

It wasn't any good for the lumber yard to have a bunch of broke builders and tradesmen starving for lack of business acumen. So, the lumberyard itself began running the books for them. They would look at the plans, figure the needed supplies, bid the jobs. They would deliver the materials, pay the help, collect the money from the sale, and then cut a check to the builder or tradesman. Apparently, this worked swimmingly.

Another part of his story was the shady, good old boy dealings in town. The lumber yard had its ups and downs that followed building ups and downs and logging ups and downs. There were good times when the money flowed like, well, something that flows. There were less good times when the bank loans to stay afloat were large.

It was the only building supplier in the area, so even when Dan's dad was mayor, the city bought materials there. And that was the proverbial one straw too many, and pop goes the camel back.

Some of the good old boys got a bee in their bonnets over something, and then they influenced the bank to call all the notes, and they were pretty uncallable at the time. That was the end of the lumber yard.

The property wound up with some big name in town. Big name on account of the big piles of dollars that family kept stashed away. The daughter in that family knew Dan's family business had been there and always told him she wanted him to have the property—the property erstwhile called his "campus."

Well, truth be told, the property was quite unattractive in the traditional sense, and poorly sited. She wanted him to have it because she didn't want it, more so than altruism and nostalgia, says I. And I'm pretty sure I'm right based on the price she gouged him with when she got ready to "give" him back his family's place.

That's why he had the campus when I met him. And in all that talk of building stuff and all, at some point in our storytelling the rat story came up. I hope you're happy. Because the tie-in is right here. Dan knew about the rat story. *He* had built the little chicken house.

I reread this to proofread it, maybe you assumed I hadn't. It was only then that I noticed I still hadn't told you the connection! Good thing I reread it, or you'd really blow a gasket. So here it is: after Dan told me about building the little test chicken house for the lawsuit, he said, "Well, you know that whole thing was out there somewhere on that farm where you live."

All that time, I'd known about the death and the test and the lawsuit. And Willy and Wally cheating the rodent version of the Grim Reaper. And it all happened right here on Ridgewood Farm. Wonder if the various current resident rodents ever hear chains rattling in the attic, or see ethereal lab rats walking down a certain path, or hear little rodent moans on a moonless night.

This is just the sort of thing that happens all the time with Ridgewood Farm and the original occupants. Everyone we meet seems to have a connection and a story. It started day one.

The Farmhouse Roof

New, watertight roof. Photo by Barry Brown. And this is before we got a pressure washer, if you must know. I might even get in trouble for using a photo taken when the guest house was in such dire need of a good pressure washing.

You could say the stories about the Farm started with an electrical failure. That's not exactly right, though. The electric company failed to turn the power on at the original farmhouse. Maybe the stories started with the insurance company refusing to insure the place until the farmhouse had a new roof. But better to start at the start. This really all started when my wife bought the farm.

The preceding is one of my favorite lines ever. I sometimes write articles for *Hobby Farms* magazine. Usually, I do pieces about a miserable failure on the farm that I squeaked a modest win out of.

I often try, as I have in this book, to write in such a way that reading my stuff is somewhat enjoyable. To me, that seems like humor should be included, regardless what you think of my attempts. So, one of my first articles began with, "It all started when my wife bought the farm." Because that's funny or witty or punny or something.

First thing the editor cut. Actually, he didn't cut it. That would have been better. He neutered it. "It all started when my wife bought *a* farm." Blah. I hate that my name is out there on that dribble. My wife is still alive, which makes this humor okay.

My wife bought Ridgewood Farm and moved here from Washington state. She sold a 1,400-square-foot house in the Vancouver suburbs. It had an entire lawnmower width of lawn all the way around it. All four sides! For roughly the same as the selling price there, she got forty acres of woods and farmland, the main Ridgewood Farm house, the original farmhouse built in the 1800s and now used as an AirBnb, and various farm buildings.

And true, the insurance people were insistent that the little farmhouse roof needed to be replaced. Yesterday. So, we lined up friends and family to knock it out together one Saturday. It would be a hoot.

Unroofing and reroofing a house is just the sort of crazy fun project that friends and family love to volunteer for, and then, as the day approaches, opt out of. And that's exactly what happened. Lori and I unroofed the whole house ourselves. Lori's then 86-year-old mother stacked old roofing on my trailer to haul to the dump. Her brother weather cancelled—more on that later. All my local friends and family painstakingly found other things to do.

When it came time to start reroofing, I plugged in my air compressor at the house and nothing happened. I knew what the IT guys would say, so I rebooted it (unplugged it and plugged it back in.) Nothing continued happening. I tested other outlets at the little house. Other things in the outlets. The power company had failed to turn on the power.

That's no step for a stepper, as my old frame carpentry boss used to say. I unrolled extension cords from the main house over. The air compressor still wouldn't work. Who knew all those "volt/amp drop over distance" charts on extension cord packaging were the real deal? Well, I learned they are.

Still doable. There is an equipment rental place literally across the street. I went over to rent a generator so we could get to gun-nailing some roofing down. The old man at the counter said, "Where are you taking our generator?" When I pointed, he got all excited. And then he shared our first Ridgewood Farm story.

When he was a young teenager, his family had moved here from Kentucky. The original owner of Ridgewood Farm was a state senator, lawyer, and judge. He had hired this teenage boy back in the 1950s to do odd jobs around the farm. This fella had nothing but good things to say about the judge. Story after story about him doing everything in his power to help this or that person get justice.

The judge had also invited him to ride horses at the farm on occasion, which is the source of another interesting tidbit from the rental company family.

The old man and his son run the equipment rental company. It doesn't seem overly busy, and there's always a huge screen television blaring a ballgame or news. I think it just might be a getaway for them. Like a cross between a family business and a man-cave.

Well, after we had been at the farm a couple of years and were selling square hay bales every year, this one year the old man's daughter came with a bunch of kids to get hay for a hayride. She said she was so happy to see the farm again and regaled me with tales of riding horses with the original farm owner. I shared this story with her brother the next time I rented a piece of equipment. He said his sister was batty and had never ridden a horse in her life.

So even though everyone had a story about the farm and its owners, some of them might have been … exaggerated. Or not. I don't know. The way my memory has been lately, even the ones I'm sharing might be suspect.

Now that I think about it, this wasn't the first connection story we encountered at Ridgewood Farm. But I had said, "More on this later," about my wife's brother.

Davis Air

Original photo: Percuzz_capt | Shutterstock. Artistically altered by Barry Brown.

When we set the plans to reroof the guest house immediately after purchasing Ridgewood Farm, Lori's brother said he would fly in and help. He has volunteered to fly in for this or that reason a number of times.

When some people talk about flying in, they mean they'll go get a ticket, get on a proper airplane, and get to where they're going. By riding. When he says he'll fly in, he means he'll fly in. He means he'll no-kidding fly in, fly like in his own plane fly.

Sounds great, really. Just hop in the plane and go where you want. Faster than driving. No messy delays and security and what to do about parking or catching a ride like you'd have flying on an airline.

But flying isn't always what it's cracked up to be.

I was in high school when Top Gun came out. The first time. It was the first movie I remember where people had some kind of geek contest about how many times they had seen it. That was a bigger deal then because every time you saw it, you were watching it in a theater. The theater was showing it along with maybe four or five other options. That's it. You couldn't watch it at home or on your phone or the computer you didn't have yet.

It was also interesting for me because I had a friend who had actually lived there because his dad had been an instructor at Miramar at the Top Gun school. We'd sit and watch the movie—huh, this must have been after VCRs came out, because I watched it at their house. Anyway, we'd sit and watch the movie and they would point out who was a real person, as in not an actor, but an actual personnel member at the base.

I have gotten off track. The main point I was thinking about getting to was that Top Gun was career day for every high school male for about half a decade. We all simply *had* to be fighter pilots. I mean, how could you blame us? Our options were Jedi knight, getting the bejeezies beat out of us by Russian boxers, or Cuban coke drug lord, dying friendless and stoned. Vietnam hero was out of the question since the war was over. Surely you can see that fighter pilot was all we had.

All it took to change our minds were facts. First, the fact that you have to score well on military entrance exams. That disqualified most of my friends. And not smoke pot. That got a handful. And have perfect vision. That got the rest of us.

Even so, this was one of my first opportunities later in life to see what Hollywood does to us. The movie gave us the idea that being a fighter pilot is mostly about flying around acrobatically and dogfighting. All the time. Interspersed with episodes of having hot chicks fall in love with you whether you've showered or can form a sentence or not.

The air wings of our military still practice dog fighting. They do this—unlike most countries—because we have more dollars than sense for the wasted time and fuel. The last dogfights were over FIFTY years ago. Then TWENTY-FIVE years ago, we shot down a few planes in Iraq. From miles and miles away with missiles. Not dog-fighting.

Then we destroyed the greatest part of Saddam's air force by bombing the piss out of it where he tried to hide it on the ground. Not super glorious, fighter-pilot-wise.

But more inglorious than that is the actual life of a fighter pilot. Once you're in the plane, you have a couple of hours of fuel. If you cruise along without doing anything fun. Whooping around dog-fighting and busting off in afterburner burns fuel faster than dumping it out a hole in the bottom of the plane.

Most of your time nowadays is spent flying in circles back and forth to the refueler plane, hoping like hell the enemy will be dumb enough to take a plane off over there a hundred miles away so that you can lob a missile at it and celebrate with your buddies at the bar afterwards.

But even that isn't most of your time. Fighter pilots show up for work—when they work—at some godawful, non-existent time in the morning. Then they sit around talking about what they're going to do first. Briefings about the situation, the weather, the enemy, the enemy's friends and family, the plan, the alternate plan, the contingency plans. For hours.

Then fly for an hour or so.

Then back to the classroom to talk again. Talk about what you did, how you did it, why you did it, what you could do differently. Twelve hours of not flying for every hour in the air going in circles.

And, is it okay if I keep going? It isn't exciting even if something exciting almost happens. Hollywood isn't there filming.

I was deployed to a place I'm not sure if we're allowed to tell yet. The pilots flew a bunch of circles, hoping the enemy would take off. They invited all the rest of us to their debrief sessions one day because they had gotten to blow some stuff up on the ground. Or the Brits with them had, I can't remember.

I swear it was like watching the slowest, most boring three or four dots on a screen imaginable. No video. No audio. Just these crazy goobers jumping around trying to impress the rest of us with what they said was really going on.

Pilots are great people. I'm super glad they're on my side. They serve an important purpose. So do plumbers. I just don't want to be one of either. Still on the fence about farming.

I got lost a while there. I was saying flying isn't always what it's cracked up to be. I was saying that because it isn't.

Lori and her brother jokingly call him and his plane Davis Air. Motto: when you absolutely don't have to be there on time. Or get there at all. Because that is what happens most of the time.

I am weather-conscious. Livestock need liquid water. Not ice. Rain and storms are no-nos when making hay. What one does in the garden, what one hauls in an open trailer, plans for outdoor work around the farm, burn piles and prescribed burning of hay fields. All weather dependent.

But Davis Air. I swear if there's a weather anomaly in Guatemala, Davis Air is grounded. Your basic normal weather considerations like sun, rain, and wind are not all that must be considered.

If a butterfly flaps its wings in Point Nemo, the most remote place on earth (look it up) and that little poof of wind wafts a dandelion seed which lands on a teeter-totter and, well, I really don't know how you're supposed to do this butterfly flapping business, but you get the point. Somehow, it results in a squall of insurmountable ferocity at the exact altitude Davis Air flies or something.

The main gist is that Davis Air absolutely cannot be relied upon. Not like you can rely on getting Ridgewood Farm stories out of every Tom, Dick, and Harry you run into. Which takes us back to the first connection story we heard.

The Realtor

The Drapes. Photo by Barry Brown.

When my wife decided to move here from Washington state, she started playing around on Zillow. Zillow is the real estate version of Pinterest. Pinterest is the bane of men.

When your woman is on the intrerwebs, and gets on the Pinterest, she will find all this crap that other people have done. Turning junk into cute things, remodeling this, rebuilding that. She will start—but not finish—projects. The house will get full of poster paint and popsicle sticks. Pinecones and glitter glue. Busted kitchen appliances.

Then, halfway through trying to make a bas relief of the Mona Lisa out of old dirt dauber nests and fruit roll-ups, she'll decide it's too hard and tell you that you need to finish it. It was photoshopped in the first place. It is not finishable.

Women get addicted to Pinterest and start using the word "just" a lot. As in, "you could *just* repurpose a bunch of cheap antique wooden windows from Facebook Marketplace and build me a Florida room out of them, like this:" showing you an obviously altered photo of some Taj Mahal-looking edifice, gleaming in the morning sun. White wicker furniture and throw pillows galore. Looks like someone spent a mint compressing an entire issue of *Better Homes & Gardens* into one small sunroom.

On Zillow, it's all about the next place "we could live." Nothing practical, affordable, or remotely appealing. "We could *just* fix up this old castle, half sunk into this malarial cesspool swamp, it would be great!" or "I bet no one thought of remodeling this shut-down toxic chemical plant into a place to live!"

So, my wife decided to move to Arkansas and started searching on Zillow. Fortunately, she avoided the old chemical plant, and there weren't any castles listed at that time. The chemical plant got remodeled into a church—I swear I'm not making this up. Her two main choices were Ridgewood Farm and an unnamed place on Gum Springs Road.

There were plenty of places listed, of course, and just about everything listed was in the right price range if you're selling a tiny home in Washington state to fund the purchase. She was still working in Washington and sent me to investigate. I took Ellie.

Before you get all judgy that here I was taking some chick to look at homes my girlfriend was interested in buying, know that Ellie is my dog. I got her in unusual circumstances. For me.

There was this couple I had befriended. They were on hard times. They no-kidding lived in a shed. With no water or electricity. They spent lots of time visiting nearby businesses for potty breaks, and used a car battery to charge cell phones. I hired them to help me on a couple of jobs, and they felt beholden to me, as really old people used to say.

One evening, my doorbell went off. I opened the door to these two standing there.

"We brought you a puppy," the gal said. The fella just stood there fidgeting like he couldn't wait long till his next visit to the meth dealer. That was not a metaphor.

This is why I said I got Ellie under unusual circumstances. There are gifts you don't give without asking first, like puppies, reptiles, babies, anything alive, really. I was quite upset at first. But Ellie quickly grew on me. Well, *growing* on me wasn't what she did first.

What she did first happened while I was lying on my back in bed. Ellie was there on my tummy, staring happily at me as I talked with Lori on the phone about this inappropriate gift. And then, as we're listing inappropriate gifts, Ellie gave me one. That explosive, wormy diarrhea that all puppies tend to have. She blasted it all down the front of me.

And smiled.

I named her Eleison. "What the hell for?" you ask. So judgy. Eleison is "have mercy" in Greek. As in *Kyrie Eleison* by Mr. Mister. I was at a point where I thought some mercy could definitely get had in my

Ellie, looking like a fruit bat. Photo By Barry Brown.

Fruit bat, looking like Ellie. Courtesy of The Concersation, Subphoto/Shutterstock.

immediate vicinity. I called her Ellie for short.

My wife had experience in animal welfare and assured me Ellie didn't look like a chi-weenie, as the couple told me. She said Ellie was definitely a Brünhund. Try as I might, I couldn't find anything online about Brünhunds.

That's because, jokes on me, that's the animal welfare term for mutt that makes them sound special and more adoptable.

Lori only told me this was a stupid, made-up name for morons after I had tried to sound wise and knowing all over town. Telling everyone within earshot that Ellie might look like a chi-weenie, or a fruit bat, but I had it on good authority that she was actually a Brünhund.

Ellie and I hopped in the truck—I hopped, I had to put Ellie on the console where she liked to ride. She was too short to hop into the truck. When we got to the farm, she flew through the fields. She had the time of her life. She bounded.

You know an animal is really getting it when they bound.

Ellie with wristwatch for size comparison Photo by Barry Brown.

Eventually, my wife made it out to see Ridgewood Farm and the Gum Springs Road property. Believe me, the farm was the better choice.

The Gum Springs place was much newer, but pretty sparse in the tree department. In Arkansas, the summer shade is critical if you're into not dying. And not having to sell organs on the black market to pay the electric bill.

It was also weird in an uncomfortable way. I started this book by saying places have souls. That house suggested "serial killer" or something. Not in a scary, haunted, sinister way. Hard to explain. In a quiet, suggestion sort of way.

As we walked through the house, questions just kept arising, like, "Why would you have a goofy little room like *this*?" or "Where do you think this hallway was supposed to go?" There were ceilings of odd heights and strange ways you had to go through one room to get to another. It just seemed the sort of place Norman Bates' mom could rock her rocking chair in, or where bodies could be hidden.

We quickly returned to look at Ridgewood Farm. And—here comes the first farm-related connection story—the realtor looked around in the great room at the end of the house. She squinted her eyes a bit and said, "Ehh, I think I remember these curtains."

The great room, as we call it, sits at the east end of the ground floor. Apparently, it wasn't part of the original plan. In the process of building the house, the judge's wife came out and saw it. She told him she wouldn't be living in that thing as long as it looked lop-sided. I guess she had been looking at the 1950s version of Pinterest. Maybe back then it was called *Better Homes & Gardens*.

Incidentally, did you know that *Better Homes & Gardens* is out of Des Moines, Iowa? Did you ever think of Des

Moines, or anywhere else in Iowa, for that matter, as being a trend-setter for style and décor? I mean, style and décor that doesn't involve livestock or denim?

Back to the story, the judge's wife wouldn't live in something so indecorous as to be unsymmetrically lopsided, but linoleum flooring in the great room was okay. Oak hardwood throughout the rest of the house. But linoleum for crying out loud. Because *that's* stylish. So the great room had to be added on to make the house appear symmetrical.

The realtor says, "Yeah, I'm sure I remember these curtains. I sewed them when I was here in college." So—my estimate, or maybe she told me—around 35-40 years earlier, as a college home economics major, she was commissioned to make curtains that still hung in the main house at Ridgewood Farm.

As a side note, my wife initially said those curtains would be the absolute first thing to go. First, like before emptying-the-trash-left-in-the-trash-can first. Then they grew on her and they're still here. As is the linoleum. Waiting for me to get time to replace it with flooring I purloined.

The Projects

Mini-French doors. Photo by Barry Brown

Searcy's university, née college, Harding University, A.D. 1925-present, is growing. Physically. Back thirty-five years ago or so, the campus didn't need to be nearly so large.

The reason college campuses used to be smaller, was that dormitories were smaller. Dormitories were smaller because the rooms were smaller. Years ago, dormitory rooms were designed in Tokyo or somewhere like that where space is a premium. In my college dorm room, I remember either my roommate or I could do situps in the floor, but not both. This is not an exaggeration.

Also, amenities were considerably less luxurious back then. My dorm had blocks of eight rooms, two guys each, sharing a bathroom. Four sinks, two commodes, and two showers. For sixteen guys. Nowadays, even high security prison inmates have better accommodations.

College dormitories nowadays have a couple of guys roughing it in a suite with a square footage that young newlyweds dream about. A bath shared by four guys. Life is easier when you're waiting for your morning constitutional behind three guys not 15.

As dormitories grow larger, the campuses have to grow larger. So, Harding is bulldozing old houses and beautiful pecan trees as fast as the development team can talk the little old ladies that own them into signing them over in their wills.

As worried as you were about Frank and Dan and the rats, I bet you're chomping at the bit for the tie-in here. Well, simmer down. Before Lori even moved here, she was plotting remodeling plans for the main house. And the cheesy vinyl flooring in the great room was an early target.

Thus it was, that when I heard via the grapevine that Harding was about to bulldoze a couple of little old lady houses on the fringes of campus, I went into action. Cue Mission Impossible theme.

The person who told me had gotten permission to raid something in one of the houses prior to demolition. Free for the taking. I knew the houses were of a vintage that surely had oak flooring.

I went to the head of the maintenance department and asked. They practically peed themselves fretting over liability. Super easy fix if you're into fixing things. Finally talked them into letting me yank out the flooring. Lots of hand-shaking and poo-pooing litigious persons.

"Yank out the flooring" doesn't do justice to the amount of work involved. Every board was nailed to the subfloor around 300 times. The flooring boards were a couple of inches wide. I crowbarred and pried. I yoinked and hammered. I filled trailer after trailer and stacked the flooring in an empty space in Dan's campus, as it turned out. To get the amount of square footage I needed for the Ridgewood Farm great room, I cleaned almost all the flooring out of three little houses.

I had to finish before the wrecking crews started. I was behind and fearing I wouldn't get enough. I hired a special needs assistant. He managed to break several of my tools and step on a nail. All the way through the sole of his shoe and much of his foot. Bled like a stuck pig.

That was in 2019. Those boards are still at Dan's, waiting for me to figure out how to use them to redo the great room floor.

That is not the worst project here. But there have been successes. I already told you about the guest house roof. That went rather well, all told. Another smashing success was the redo of the den in the main house.

Antique Searcy business door. Note the unusual visible facing of the hinges. Photo by Barry Brown.

When Lori bought Ridgewood Farm, there were lots of odd things that we discovered here and there and everywhere. There were bits and pieces of horse tack. See what I did there? Bits? Anyway, there were political signs for electoral races at local, state, and national levels. And there were doors.

One door in particular was larger than normal, and almost entirely glass, having wood for about a foot at the top and bottom, and six to eight inches on the sides. The glass was that beautiful, wavy, poured antique glass. The brass hinges were unlike any I'd seen. Half was hidden between the edge of the door and the jamb, but the other half was attached to the front of the door where it was always visible.

The den when Lori bought the place had two openings toward the main bits of the downstairs. Just openings. No doors. No way to close off the noise of the kitchen or dining room.

I decided to put that huge door in one opening. The opening and the door were not the same size, naturally. And the amount I needed to remove from the door was too great to take it all from the wood. It would have left sides that were only two to three inches of wood. So I disassembled the door, cut the antique glass down without breaking it, and put it back together.

I said, I cut the antique glass without breaking it.

That is the most phenomenal thing you'll read in this book, and you went through it like it was nothing.

Since that time, strolling downtown we've seen several original old storefronts with the same unique style door and hinges. This one must have been on a downtown office or storefront downtown and got shoved in a barn here on the farm during a remodel.

That left one doorless opening in the den. I didn't want a big door swinging into the room and being in the way all the time. I wanted two narrow doors that could swing open and NOT be in the way all the time.

There is a name for this type of door that escapes me. It isn't French door, because those are typically filling a double wide opening, as each door is a more normal width. I found a few for sale, but they'd been pulled out of really old fancy houses in New Orleans and were weird heights and thousands of dollars over my budget.

I found tons of old, used solid wood doors online. And when I say used, I mean five doors for twenty bucks used. I wound up taking a few of those and disassembling them, whittling the various pieces down, and reassembling. They were normal all-wood doors, so I took out the upper panels and replaced them with glass. They turned out great. Now you can close the doors and retreat into the den and write a book or something. Trust me.

Besides paint and new outlet and switch covers, the other main den change is the "built-in" bookcases. They aren't really built-in, FYI.

Lori loves this online auction bunch. One benefit is that you don't have to leave the house, if you're her. You just bid on stuff and then send your husband to go pick up whatever you won. Like bookcases.

The auction company assists people moving to assisted care. They sell real estate, auction off butt-loads of hoarded stuff, and actually help people physically move to their new home.

The house where Lori won the bookcases, three in number, was on a dirt cattle track that wound its way off a major four-lane highway in Little Rock. Four plus a turn lane. The dirt track was smack in a hairpin curve. The bookcases were so large I had to take a trailer.

It was all I could do to get onto the dirt track, what with four lanes of rushing traffic racing all around me with the posted speed limit at 45 miles per hour. Then once I did, I realized I might have screwed up.

You may have felt this before if you've ever driven with a trailer. Up a dirt cattle trail. "How will I ever get out of here?" you ask yourself. "Will I have to BACK back out of this windy piece of—" well, you get the point. Backing out would have also meant backing onto a four-lane highway with oncoming traffic I couldn't see around the hairpin curve. And all of them over the speed limit.

I stopped smack in the dirt cattle path driveway. I thought if I had to back out, I might as well not make it worse. I walked up the rest of the way to the house.

At which house, I kid you not, there were already three trucks, one with a trailer, plus all the cars of the people working the auction. In a domestic parking area meant for one car, a four-wheeler, and maybe one of those Fred and Barney Little Tykes plastic cars toddlers move along with their feet.

I helped load out the other guys with trucks and the one with the trailer and pulled up closer. It was like one of those slidy-tile puzzles trying to get out of the way enough for the other guys to get out. Then forward and reverse 306 times to get turned around and aimed back out of the driveway. The workers informed me that whoever got the bookcases had to take the books on them. The books filled every shelf about three books deep. So, we started loading books into boxes.

The boxes filled the inside of the truck, the bed of the truck, and then we stacked boxes beside the trailer to put in the bookcase spaces once they were loaded.

It took three grown men to load each of the three bookcases. Then, in went the remaining boxes of books. And I took off for home. It's so easy for her to buy stuff at these auctions.

The bookcases were natural, solid oak. I painted the front trim boards white and left the shelves and insides natural wood. I removed the quarter-round and baseboard from the wall behind where they were meant to go and put them against the wall. I matched the quarter-round and baseboard to the sides of the bookcases, and ran crown molding around the top of all three bookcases together. The result— for all appearances—is a three-banger built-in bookcase.

The rest of the main house is a project waiting to happen. The guest house, though, has my current magnum opus.

The Guest House Porch

New guest house porch. Photo by Barry Brown The old porch was so ugly and dangerous, the photo wouldn't render, and even the photo could have injured someone..

When the home inspector saw the guest house porch, he said something like, "Your insurance company isn't going to like that." When the insurance guy saw the guest house porch, he said, "I don't like that." I mean, that's approximately what happened. It's been seven years now.

The guest house main entry was about four feet off the ground, necessitating stairs and a porch for all but professional athletes, of which we have about zero staying here.

The porch and stairs looked like old barn wood: gray, weathered, slick, and a poor anchor point for nails or screws. The sides of the porch had no rails. Thus, guests on the porch could easily fall four feet off any of the three sides that weren't up against the house.

The stairs themselves did have a rail on one side. It wasn't anchored to anything, so it had a lot of give to it. In other words, it might look okay in your staged photographs, but for the love of all that's good, please don't *actually lean* on it to catch your fall.

The roof above the porch was designed by the aesthetically challenged. It was cheesy green see-through fiberglass corrugated roofing. Quite possibly the ugliest combination imaginable. In fact, I don't believe you could come up with an uglier roof material. The roof was built at an angle that blocked the view of half the door, or interfered with the view of someone standing on the porch looking out.

I knew we needed a new porch. If I hadn't known on my own, Lori was happy to remind me. Frequently.

In fact, here's the chronology. Pre-COVID, Lori said, figure out what it would cost to build a new porch and deck. I did. Lori saw the figure and said let's put this off. Then she saw an older guest trying to navigate the steps and meander into the door, often swaying perilously close to the edge.

Figure out what it would cost to do that porch and deck, she said again. This was amidst the COVID shutdown. And by "shutdown" in this story, I mean the portion when the lumber industry all went home, and wood products had to be sourced from dwarves who hand-carved 2x4s out of magic trees that grew under some diamond mountain guarded by fire-breathing dragons or something. The price was over four times my original estimate. Lori saw the figure and said let's put this off.

I could bore you with the back-and-forth that occurred subsequently, but I'm going to assume you're bright enough to figure it out. Suffice to say, it was rather a lot of back and quite a bit of forth.

Part of the problem was my hesitation to act. When I hit a baffler of a problem, I sort of table it for later, hoping a solution will present itself. In this case, it was how to make the porch line up right. I wanted the roof line to match the existing back side of the roof. I wanted the porch to be horizontal enough nothing rolled off. I wanted a wheelchair access ramp. I hoped for square and level.

The zinger was putting a porch post in the ground, in cement, such that fourteen feet in the air or so the top end would line up where it needed to. To match the back roof, the back wall, and the side wall of the house—none of which it actually touched. I couldn't figure that out. It involved a lot of air measurements. So, I waited.

Six years later, Lori's demands to BUILD the porch were outstripping her demands to NOT BUILD the porch. It helped that she got a really high bid from a contractor, and she thought she could save money if she made me do it. She absolutely loves saving money by having me do stuff.

I measured and eyeballed and strung line and pondered. I pick-axed the solid granite and kryptonite out of six holes and set the posts. Figuring that was a good start, I got back to waiting.

I was still way up in the air with nothing to measure to and no plan for how to make the rafters work. At least I had started. That's something I learned from my dad. No fear.

Fear is what keeps those of you who wish you could "build a deck" or "take out this wall" or "fix the car" from doing it. Fear that you don't know what you're doing. Fear that you'll mess something up.

I don't know what I'm doing any more than you do, and I'm just as likely to mess something up. Probably more likely. But what I learned growing up was to not *fear* that. Just tear off into a project. What can it hurt? I can always walk to work if I screw up the car. I can cover up mess-ups with caulk and paint. The house is insured, toss in a Molotov cocktail and break out the weenies and marshmallows.

It helped on this project that I know great people who do great things. That's how I solved the rafter problem. Thanks, Ben. Your beautiful deck-building projects gave me the ideas I needed.

No fear, knowing good people. Maybe being flexible, too. Have a loose plan, ready to alter as needed.

The porch turned out great. The ramp turned out great. I'm now waiting on decent weather to complete the deck around the front of the house. One day.

But I've gotten off track. We were talking about everyone we run into having a connection or story about Ridgewood Farm. Like my eye doctor of all people. Not the one now, the one I had as a little kid.

The Ophthalmologist

Photo courtesy of TV Guide.

I hope I've used the right term. There are lots of "O" words out there, and I have no intention of switching to my internet to check myself when the world is full of fact checkers. I did use the spell checker to fix how I had it spelled once I saw the squiggly line under it. I mean, look at that nonsense. There's no way we should have a word like that.

If I don't have it right, I'll explain. I don't mean the one who fools around with teeth. Or braces. Or just fits the glasses to your face. Or sets broken bones. Or gives people the bad news about their cancer. Or watches birds. So many "O" words out there. Also, not the one who just figures out what glasses you need. I'm talking about the one who did all of med school and can whack around on your eye with a knife. Legally.

My vision is trash. Without glasses, I can't tell you what I can see, because I can't make anything out. I think I was in about second grade when Mom took me to the eye doctor. I don't remember why she knew this needed to be done.

I do remember why Dad went to the eye doctor as a kid. That story—not first person, heard it from others—is that he made it through quite a bit of school without having the foggiest idea that there was stuff written on the board. When the teacher called on him, he thought he was supposed to recite whatever the kid before him said, so he did. Apparently, that only works for so long till you are supposed to "say" (read) something other than what the other kid did. Then you get caught.

Whatever the reason for me, I remember not thinking the eye doctor's office was a pleasant place to be. Must have been a kid thing. I know my eye doctor and his wife now, and they're great.

As a kid, the office carpet and paneling were too dark, there were too many unknown pieces of scary-looking equipment, and the whole place might have smelled funny.

An assistant put us in an exam room. Mom sat down and put her handbag by her chair. On the side by the door.

"Oh!" the assistant threw her hands to her face, "Ma'am! You can't put your bag there! The doctor will trip over it."

Mom thought she was kidding, and didn't think it was the greatest of jokes. But the lady moved the purse a bit. As it turns out, not only was she serious, she had not moved it far enough. The doctor stumbled all over it anyway.

My eye doctor—the O whatever—was very tall and thick. A little duh-huh-ish as well. Like a normal-colored Herman Munster without the sunken eyes. And wearing Buddy Holly glasses.

I know what he looked like because in the course of his exam, he got close. Very close. I don't think I've ever been so close to another man, and I've been in Tokyo subways.

There we'd be, faces squashed together as he looked through some kind of lighthouse search beacon into my eye going, "Hmm, mmm hmm, hmm." And the whole, "Which one seems brighter and clearer, number one or number two," that any glasses wearer is familiar with.

That part of the story has nothing to do with Ridgewood Farm, as you can well see. But many years later, my parents got into this phase of an eating rotation after Sunday church services.

Sounds like I got *farther* from Ridgewood Farm, doesn't it? Shows what you know. Well, every Sunday after church, they'd go out to eat and invite me. Country Kitchen, Chinese buffet, Mexican—I think Los Tucanos and the place in the hotel that went out of business—the hospital cafeteria, maybe

Western Sizzlin', I can't remember for sure. Then start the rotation over again.

Certain places were off limits. E.g. any place that had its liquor license. As a small child, Mom had helped care for alcoholic relatives. "Care for" meaning physically support them in the bathtub so they wouldn't drunkenly slip underwater and drown. Or clean up vomit when they'd gotten drunk despite being on Antabuse. Dad had dealt with a father who was abusive when on binges. The solution was to be personally teetotalling, politically teetotalling, religiously teetotalling, and fiscally teetotalling. I don't have to agree, but I won't blame.

The hospital cafeteria was a surprisingly good option on the rotation. They had a couple of entrées to choose from, good sides, and a very good pay-by-weight salad bar.

I am not above making things up for a good story. But this is not the time. Frank and my eye doctor and his wife ate lunch together Sundays at the hospital. So, we saw them all regularly. This was forty-plus years after my initial visit to the eye doctor's office, and thirty-plus years since I had even seen him and his wife.

Sometimes we even sat with them. Frank didn't have anything new to add to the Ridgewood Farm story. He had gotten pretty hard of hearing and foggy of mind by then. But not my eye doctor.

I keep saying "my eye doctor" because apparently I've gotten a little foggy of mind myself. That's the best I can do. Maybe his name will come to me later.

Anyway, he and his wife asked where I was living. I told him I was on Ridgewood Farm. Boy, did he get excited. Almost as excited as the time we sat with him when Frank wasn't there.

I guess without Frank there he felt free to ask about him. Bill! There's his name! I knew it would come to me. Well, it isn't really Bill because I'm changing names here. I just remembered that's the name I wanted to use for him. Regardless the name, he still looked like a massive cross between Herman Munster and Buddy Holly

Anyway, so Bill and Frank used to go to the Methodist church, and then Frank switched to my parents' church. And that really threw Bill for a loop.

Bill asked why Frank did that. And did they do something wrong to him at the Methodist church? Then he started expressing a lack of understanding about my folks' church.

Now when my people start to express misunderstanding, it is aimed more at the other person directly. As in, "I don't understand how *ya'll* can ..." Bill was so much softer, so much less direct. There was no "ya'll" in his expression.

Apparently, a lady who was a university professor had given a presentation at Bill's church on some Bible topic or other. He was quite impressed with her knowledge and ability to share it. He had told her that her church—same as my parents'—was very fortunate to have such a knowledgeable person who could share such insights. She informed him that she didn't share that information at her church.

Because she wasn't allowed to.

And that baffled Bill, as it should. But he didn't say, "I don't understand why *ya'll* do that." Or "you all" if that's what bugs you about his statement. Or "Y'uns."

117

All he said was, "That's fascinating. I don't understand that."

But I digress. Again.

That was a time when Frank wasn't there, and I remember because Bill was curious about why Frank moved churches. I think Frank moved for business reasons, truth be told. When over half the town goes to one location or another of the same denomination, it doesn't hurt business to have your religious sentiments adjust accordingly.

But it was a time Frank *was* there that Bill mentioned a connection with Ridgewood Farm.

Sailing

Original AI-generated image courtesy of Freepik. Artistically modified by Barry Brown.

As I was saying, when Bill found out I lived at Ridgewood Farm, he got excited. He had known the original owner years before and spent a bit of time with him.

The original owner had various law-related occupations. He had been an attorney, a judge, and a state senator. Thus, some people referred to him as judge, and some as senator. Maybe he had been in the state house of representatives as well. Seems like someone called him congressman or representative.

Bill was younger than the judge. The judge would give him a call to come over. He'd pour up the scotch and they'd share a few, then take off for the lake. This was back when America was wild and loose. When you could knock back a few stiff drinks and drive to the lake without anyone getting snooty about it. Maybe it's the same way today if you're a big-time politician and judge.

We live in a dry county. For those of you who think I'm referring to the climate, let me disabuse you of that misconception. I don't know the history of dry counties. I'll leave that to the fact checkers, again. But dry counties across the South are those in which alcohol cannot be sold. Not in restaurants, not in liquor stores, not in bars, of which naturally there are none. Without alcohol, bars lose appeal.

There was always some kind of weird exception for private clubs. I guess the private nature of them made them something like a private home. Even in the nominally free America we live in, authorities haven't yet stepped off into telling us we can't have alcohol in our homes. So, I can always remember a mysterious alcohol-fogged zone of drinking freedom: the country club on one end of town that served the wealthy, and the VFW on the other end of town that catered to everyone else.

Searcy is divided along strict lines. Those who support this being a dry county and those who oppose. These lines traditionally followed those who have some tie to the university, and those who don't.

Superficially, the university, née college, in its profound religiosity, is an alcohol-opposing entity. Potential staff members must swear not to consume alcohol to even be considered for hire. Unless there is a dearth of their particular area of expertise.

The university insists that all faculty and staff are teetotallers and members in good standing of the denomination the school represents. Unless they can't find someone who meets those criteria. Then the job searchers mysteriously remove from the listing those requirements for application. Apparently, these are "soft" requirements.

Alcohol consumption and one's membership in another denomination—or no church membership at all, God forbid—are strict rules for the Almighty, but ones He understands in His grace to be bendable by His institutions as needed.

The rest of the community is markedly less teetotalling, and goes to church if, where, and when they like.

Thus it was, that whenever it returned to the ballot whether the county would stay alcohol-free, a high percentage of university faculty, staff, alumni, and associated persons voted to remain dry. But it was always close. Too close for teetotalling comfort. Right up until the unfortunate demise of Harry.

Harry was a great guy. He drove a moped all over town when no one else did. It wasn't just mopeds, no one much drove motorcycles either. Motorcycles were a slippery slope that ended in being a murderous, drunken, dope-dealing Hell's Angel, I think. That's how the reasoning goes.

But it is the country. Dirt bikes were exempt, best I could tell.

Harry was the backbone of all things youth in town. He was why we had Little League baseball. He helped implement youth soccer. Youth football. Youth basketball. He coached. He molded little minds. Harry was a guy everyone liked, and to my knowledge no one had any problem with him. Ever.

And he was hit and killed on that moped by a drunk driver.

Well, that opened up a whole can of craziness. We got a MADD chapter in town, first of all. And Harry's death garnered lots of support for MADD and overall dry-ness as tee-totallers stayed tee-totalling, and some other people changed teams for the next few voting opportunities.

More recently, the state overrode the local decision by granting a liquor license to someone or other who applied here. Rumor has it — again, I have no intention of researching this — that the state passed a law that if a proprietor asked for a liquor license and the city council didn't vote it down in three consecutive meetings, they got their license by default. That put the ball in the court of city council persons.

City council members do it for a reason. They must like counciling. Or councilling. I'm not sure which, and neither is Microsoft Word based on the plethora of red squiggly lines in the last two sentences. So, council members don't want to take a stand voting for or against something the populace is divided 50-50 on. The result is that any place that has asked for a license finds the request tabled for three months, and then their license is more or less automatically granted.

No liquor stores yet, but any restaurant that wants now serves booze. You go through the motions of signing up to be a member of their "club" at some, some have even skipped that. I've asked a friend on the police force — how's that for research — and he said there hasn't been an appreciable uptick in drunk driving or pugilism or serenading Irish ballads or lawn-peeing or other alcohol-related criminal activity, thank God.

Back from the alcohol and dry county tangent. We were talking about the judge getting all liquored up and taking people sailing.

There were a few people who shared stories about sailing with the judge. I guess he really liked it. Dan and some of his friends told me that when they were high school kids the judge would call them like the post office — rain, shine, sleet, hail, tempest, or typhoon—to go sailing. No fear apparently. Which we've ascertained in the construction and maintenance world can be a good thing. I am less convinced that it is a great idea out in a sailboat on a lake in Arkansas where presumably the rescue possibilities are limited. And after a few snorts of scotch.

I'll warn you ahead of time that this next comment is totally tangential. Even for me. I did have a friend who got a DUI and a BUI the same day. "What's a BUI?" you might ask. Boating.

This was Daryl. Daryl was on a construction crew with me. I framed houses one summer of college and every member of that crew was a character in and of himself. There were no herselves on that crew. And this was long before the option to have they/them/theirselves or whatever else we're up to.

Daryl had to smoke. I was still nineteen and Daryl was a couple of years older. But without a cigarette in his actual mouth at any given moment, he physically quivered.

There you'd be, more than two-stories up, holding one end of the ridge board. The ridge board is the top line of the roof that the sloping sides go up to attach to. It's as long as the whole roof. So, you've got one end and you're waiting on the crew to start nailing rafters to it to hold it in place. And it starts wiggling on you.

It's unusual for a board to go to wiggling on its own. The uncanny nature of it makes you turn around to see what has led to this anomaly. There's Daryl, holding the other end and quivering. Like he all of a sudden caught the palsy or Parkinson's right then. I learned though. "Daryl, get a cigarette," I'd say. He would set the ridge board on his shoulder, whup out a

Marlboro red and fire it up, and then hold the board like his end was set in cement. Not making this up.

I only worked with that crew one summer. And in that one summer, Daryl got four DUIs. And the one BUI. We'd learn about it all on a Monday.

We usually got to work at some ridiculous, third-world workday-beginning time like five a.m., and there would be no Daryl. Long about ten or so, here he would come—fire up the polygraph, I'm ready—in a sky blue 1970s Monte Carlo. When the boss would holler down asking why he was late, he'd mope, "Durn cops busted me again."

But that one time he beat his high score. He had been on the lake with his ski boat. Loaded it back on the trailer and left.

Without strapping it to the trailer, in his zeal to be drunk.

When he approached the first stop sign on his route and hit the brakes, the boat exited the trailer and passed him on the shoulder. Passing on the shoulder is not legal, but it's a boat so we'll let that slide for now. What did it know?

Daryl got out of his truck and was scratching his big dumb head wondering how to get that ski boat back on the trailer when the authorities arrived.

"Whatcha been doing?" they inquired.

"I been water skiing at the lake," Daryl said, decidedly not invoking his 5th Amendment rights.

"Driving this boat?"

"Yup."

"And no passengers in this truck, which you were also driving?"

I don't have to keep on. You see where this is going. Probably some kind of record for getting a BUI when not even in the water.

Not much of the judge's sailing hobby is left but the stories. Well, the stories and the mast.

If you look closely at the purple martin house, you'll see there are no purple martins. I've tried unsuccessfully to coax some into moving in, but they're having none of it.

Now, if you continue to look closely, you might recognize the post holding the bird house up is a sailboat mast. Or you might not. I didn't. Not until Dan came by one day and said, "Will you lookit that! That's the mast to the judge's old sailboat!"

We've been all over the place in this chapter. Sailing in bad weather. Drinking as a prelude to sailing in bad weather. Dry counties. Identifying sailboat masts when there aren't birds to identify. And Daryl.

Daryl was definitely a weird critter. And weird critters are something we definitely have had at Ridgewood Farm.

The Creature

Original photo courtesy of the University of Georgia College of Agriculture & Environmental Science. Artistic modification by Barry Brown.

The first weird critter I remember encountering at the farm was called "the creature." Before you go envisioning something from the Black Lagoon or Loch Ness, let me tell you it was my three-year-old grandson that did the naming.

We have a pergola that is raised off the ground, and the dogs had started paying inordinate attention to the space beneath it. Which could mean something, or nothing, as you know if you have dogs.

Sometime into this interest in the space under the pergola, we started seeing an armadillo wandering around at night in the yard. Digging around and making a nuisance if you're into a nice lawn, which we aren't. Being rather cool if you're into animals, which we are.

I don't know if it's the armor plating or the blindness or what, but armadillos don't get overly concerned about you walking up close and looking at them. And that's how Dilly was. Lori named it Dilly if you hadn't gathered that.

We watched Dilly nightly. We watched with whomsoever was at the house when evening hit. Usually, we put the dogs inside because that made it a more peaceful, quieter, less foamy-mouthed viewing.

Our grandson happened to be at the house a lot during that time. And any time during his life, truth be told. He was away for a few days, and on his return kept asking us to see "the creature."

Of course, you know exactly what he was talking about, because that's all this story has been about so far. But we were stymied. It threw us off that a three-year-old was calling anything a "creature," and we have lots of things at the farm that he could have been talking about. The goats, the cows, the chickens, the ducks, the foxes, the coyotes, rats and mice, possums, raccoons. I could keep going. Could I, you ask? The turtles, the lizards, the frogs, the zillions of birds, the salamanders, the snakes. "The creature" did turn out to be Dilly.

But it didn't turn out to be the last "creature" by any stretch.

The First Snapping Turtle

Original photo courtesy of Herps of Arkansas. Artistic modifications by Barry Brown. I had a photo of the actual turtle we caught, but then the turtle ate my phone and the photo was thereby lost.

Ridgewood Farm has a pond. It is a small pond, but has been a source of great fun over the years. Fishing, swimming, animal watching, rock chucking. Just about everything a pond should be.

Near the beginning of our tenancy on the farm, I was curious just what all might be found in the pond. We found mussel shells on the banks. We could see sunfish and bass from the edge. Small-headed water turtles popped up for air, and snakes occasionally s-curved across making ripples. Sometimes we'd see a heron or a pair of geese. But I wanted to know if there were catfish.

Catfish is the southern equivalent of [_____] in the North: they're everywhere, they're tasty, and everyone loves them. I tried several things from snow to liberals in that sentence and couldn't find anything I was happy with, so you get a blank to fill in yourself.

I wanted catfish because Lori is very feminine. In the sense that she doesn't want fish that tastes like fish. Or eggs that taste like eggs, as we discovered with the delicacy of duck eggs later. Or alcohol that tastes like alcohol, or, well you get the point. Bream — or whatever name you know them by — tend to be fish that taste like fish. But with catfish, you can prepare them in a number of ways that might confuse the unknowing into thinking they're eating flaky white meat that came from something else.

None of our fishing had resulted in any catfish bites. I decided to get more serious. I put some liver on a hook, suspended it from a milk jug, and tossed it into the middle of the pond with a heavy string from the jug handle back to the shore.

Sure enough, the next day, the milk jug was nowhere to be found. I was just sure we had a monster catfish on the hook. I put floaties on my grandson. He had those upper-arm-mounted kind. And off we swam, following the heavy string.

There are some old posts, maybe from a now-deceased dock or fence, sticking up along one side of the pond a few feet from the shore. That was where the string was heading.

We swam over, and sure enough, the string started going down deeper around those posts. I could see the milk jug pulled under water there, so I began pulling it up. And that's when I saw the strangest thing.

Something round and white was rising to the surface. How curious.

My grandson was wallowing and bobbing along and getting close to where I was when it dawned on me what I was seeing.

There are certain things whose gaping maws appear white when they are headed toward you, or, as in this case, your unprotected fingers reaching down for the line. The aptly named Cottonmouth snake. Poisonous and mean. And the snapping turtle, less poisonous, equally mean, if not meaner.

When I was a kid, my dad used to take us fishing at a cow pond in a friend's pasture. Well, "friend" is a stretch.

It was the people who owned the local ice cream plant. They had a machine go on the blink and the manufacturer said you could only fix it by replacing a bazillion-dollar computer circuit board.

Remember how Frank liked to stick his nose in everyone's business? He wound up hearing about the problem and sending Dad to have a look.

Remember how Dad had no fear? He knew absolutely, 100 percent zero about ice cream machines. But he farted around and found the twenty-cent component on the circuit board that was bad.

The ice cream moguls were so happy. They asked what they could do for Dad, what they could pay him.

My brother and I were not present. That's why this isn't the story of how we had more free ice cream than we could ever eat the whole time we were growing up.

Dad asked if our family could fish the cow ponds at the ice cream lord's estate. And they said sure! What was a few fish, weighed against a bazillion dollars of savings on fixing ice cream machines?

What does that have to do with whatever we were talking about? It has to do with something that happened one time fishing at those ponds.

Once, Dad caught a snapping turtle there. The shell might have been the size of a dinner plate. That turtle hissed and snapped. We were a hoarding family, so Dad was not cutting the line and losing that hook. He intended to get it out of that ridiculously dangerous mouth. Well, he pulled and dodged. He tried to reach in with pliers.

Eventually, he got mad and was jabbing at the turtle's head with the butt-end of his fishing pole. That's when the power of the snapping turtle was first demonstrated for me.

That turtle snapped down on the handle of Dad's fishing pole and bit clean through it. Now, that's not impressive for the outside handle portion, which was cork for cushiony comfort. But the inside was the continuation of the fiberglass rod. In the handle, the rod was about 3/8" thick fiberglass. And that turtle snapped through it and spit it out like an earthworm, or something else you could easily bite in two and then spit out.

I have a friend I'll call Kim. She told me her grandpa said that once a snapping turtle bites down, it won't let go till there's thunder. She says she actually saw that demonstrated. Her grandpa was poking at one with his snake-scaring stick. The turtle bit down on the stick and didn't let go till her grandpa's shotgun thundered.

A 3/8" fiberglass rod is more or less the size of my finger bones, so I readily imagined that snapping turtle — back at the Ridgewood Farm pond in case you're lost — swimming up to unceremoniously chomp off my fingers.

I was concerned about spooking my grandson into drowning us both or getting us eaten by a turtle, so I said something vanilla like, "Hey, let's swim back now! Doesn't that sound fun!"

We went to my shop, took a scrap piece of metal and a broken something-handle, and fashioned a gaff. Someone had left a flat-bottomed boat by the pond, so we maneuvered it over by the turtle and got the gaff into its mouth. We pulled it up into the boat, where we had the foresight to have brought a five-gallon bucket. We didn't have the foresight to make sure the bucket was large enough.

That turtle turned out to be the diameter of the bucket. I put it in, and the shell touched both sides. It hissed and threw an absolute fit about the whole deal.

We re-homed the turtle in the river, hoping that would be a fun place to live as a scary, finger-eating menace. And also far enough away that returning to the pond was out of the question. They have no thumbs for hitchhiking, those snapping turtles. Same with owls, in case you were wondering.

The Extra-terrestrial

Original photo courtesy DavalbePendantStudio. Artistic modifications by Barry Brown.

Original photo courtesy Reddit. Modifications by Barry Brown.

One night, my daughter left here with her kids after some sort of family get-together had occurred. I mean, they hadn't been gone for thirty seconds when the phone was ringing.

"There's some kind of thing down here in the road, and you've got to see it."

That was about all we could get that made sense. Lots of whooping and hollering in the background. Descriptions that were too frantic and ADHD-riddled to mean much.

Naturally, as the animal lovers I have previously positioned Lori and myself to be, we flew into action. Pajama-covered, we dove into a non-sequitur hodge-podge of coats with fur-trimmed hoods, knee boots, and gardening gloves. We dove into the car almost like Bo and Luke Duke, then slung pine needles and leaves everywhere as we fishtailed and squalled down the driveway.

We got maybe 30 yards down the driveway, and my daughter had turned her car crossways in the road and aimed her headlights at the tree-lined edge. She had the brights searing the tree bark and hay field. Once our lights were added, there was quite a resemblance to the scene where the government weenies are doing their dead-level best to mess up E.T.'s life with search lights and hazmat suits and ample lack of understanding or heart.

And there, in the spotlight was this thing.

It was white. It was huge. Bigger-than-E.T. huge. I mean, you can actually *see* that from the example pictures at the beginning of this chapter. And it was absolutely sentient.

The reason I knew that it was sentient was that it instantly assessed the gathered crowd. And it *knew* who was most likely to mess with it.

There was my grandson, and my granddaughter, and my wife, and my daughter, whooping and yelling and hollering questions and making phone calls and taking photos. Huh. That means I should have a better photo for this chapter.

Anyway, then there's me.

I was looking at that little joker thinking, "I have got to hold that thing and pet it." That's what happens when I see anything. Non-snapping Turtle. Possum. Raccoon. Giraffe. Deer. Copperhead.

The difference between a baby great horned owl, which this turned out to be, and these other animals is that its head is clearly not connected to its body.

So being sentient, and having its head on this lazy Susan of a neck, it never stopped watching me. I circled it one way and the other, looking for a safe side to reach in and pick it up or pet it. It followed me with those monstrous owl eyes non-stop, and taunted me with razor-sharp pterodactyl talons and cigar cutter of a beak. Not a glance at the seven-year-old or two-year-old.

It being the age of cell phones, we reached out to every veterinarian, biologist, ornithologist, bird watcher, and ophthalmologist (just in case) that we could find in our contact lists.

Finally, someone responded. He said it was "just a fledgling" that the parents would look after it. And he said it sitting on the ground in our front yard alone, threatening anyone thinking about petting it was perfectly normal.

Perfectly normal.

That indicates the type of thing that occurs with some degree of regularity. And if that's truly the case, I don't know why none of you has mentioned this happening to you now and then.

But it also means I need to dig deeper if I'm going to find you an unusual story from the farm.

The Coyote

Rocket. Photo courtesy of April Watson.

Our neighbor has a dog named Rocket. Not unusual. But they were off on vacation--also not unusual—when the July 4th firework show at the Country Club up the hill behind us went off.

The neighbor man does some kind of computer blah security blah something blah dot-com for a living, and the neighbor lady teaches at the university. When they travel, she finds a student to house sit. Which they did for this trip.

So along about o-dark-thirty, this college girl called over all frantic because Rocket had vanished. And there I was thinking I might get to sleep. I didn't think he had actually Klingon-cloaking-device vanished. I was thinking more like Delmar said, he R - U - N - N - O - F - T.

I got our insanely bright searchlight flashlight and started walking. I did all our back fields. I hunted in their yard. I walked the half-mile-long fence in the front field, hoping Rocket hadn't made it to the highway at the other end.

I kept seeing red glowing Jawa eyes. Love that. You see the two dots, they watch you, then when you're close enough, the eyes turn as the deer run into the woods.

I arrived at the highway and searched up one side and back the other hoping to not find Rocket there. Then I began walking back up to the house through the fields. I saw red eyes again.

Just like in the "who's going to try to pet it" situation with the baby owl, I had to see how close I could get. I walked slowly. I stepped quietly. I even took an oblique angle in hopes it wouldn't think I was walking *at* it as a threat.

I got pretty close.

I got so pretty close that in the faint, dim edge of the circle of light peripheral to the scathing spotlight, I saw the animal whose eyes were glowing red.

And it wasn't a deer.

It was a coyote sitting at the base of a round hay bale. The story likely would have changed for many of you here. And I suppose it did for me, too. For me, it changed from, "I'm gonna see how close I can get to that deer," to "I'm gonna see how close I can get to that coyote."

Subtle, but significant change. It was a little invigorating. Zoological X-games.

After seeing that it was a coyote, I wasn't able to get much closer before it loped off toward the woods. Exhilarating! I had been *just that close* to a coyote!

Keeping chickens makes you much less fond of fauna usually. Chickens are susceptible to everything else. Possums, raccoons, foxes, hawks, owls, coyotes, dogs. I am pretty sure we even lost one to a cow, believe it or not. I think it got stepped on.

But there, a half-mile from any of our chickens, at night when they were safely locked up, I was right there with a coyote. And it was cool. For one reason, it meant Rocket probably hadn't run off this way toward the highway. Not a chance he'd have left a coyote out here in peace.

It was approximately this time when the story began to get unusual. I bet you thought it already had.

Because that's when I saw the other coyote.

I had every intention of sharing a really unusual story here. That's what the foreshadowing in the last chapter pointed to. But then I did a quick search for an appropriate photograph there at the beginning, and based on the sheer number of results, what happens in this story is a more common occurrence than I thought.

I decided to use a photo of my own. It isn't the greatest from a photography standpoint, but we aren't in a Nat Geo contest here.

Coyote on haybale. Photo by Barry Brown

The second coyote had been outside the dim edge of peripheral light. Because it was *on top* of the hay bale. These bales were four by fives, as we say in the hay and livestock business. Four feet wide by five feet in diameter, which would be five feet tall the way hay bales sit in the field.

My first thought was that the game was on again. What I had believed was my ending point of closeness with coyote number one, was only the beginning. The starting point for getting close to coyote number two.

I kept going on my slanted approach, keeping just the slightest bit of light over by the coyote. I tried to seem like I was going to walk straight by the hay bale.

That's when I noticed the unusual part. If you don't think coyotes camping out five feet in the air on hay bales is odd. And the number of online photos of them on bales suggests that's not odd.

This coyote was intentionally and actively disrespecting me. Before you get all smirky and judgy, saying I'm making stuff up, consider this. The coyote sat with its back toward me on the hay bale. Ears not alert. Not tense. It didn't change as I got closer. In fact, it took steps to disrespect me even more, even though I was clearly the alpha predator in our relationship.

This loose, limber, unconcerned coyote leaned to one side, stretched its hind leg up, and scratched its chin. You might not recognize this as an alternate version of flipping someone off, but it is. The nonchalance. The dissing. Still no eye contact.

Then it yawned. The yawn shape-shifted into a stretch. A doggy style, butt in the air, front legs to infinity and beyond, moany stretch.

And that was the point when it dropped its chin sideways in a perfect, "are you kidding me?" glance. If it had worn librarian half-glasses, it would have been looking over them. Gave itself a little shake and lithely hopped to the ground—on *my side* of the hay bale. Then it walked, not loped, not ran, not trotted, but walked, a.k.a. sauntered toward the wood line.

Infinite twinkling ink above me. Only the hint of shadowy fields reaching in every direction. Silent black boulders, the bales hid in the murk. The tree lines just a darker black border to the black world I stood in.

When I came back to myself, I thought I should measure how far away the coyote was. I began to step it off. Ten short steps not quite toe-to-toe. Maybe twelve or fifteen feet.

I will say here, because this next part is the only part my wife would want to know in this whole story, probably the whole book, Rocket was located. He had run more than two miles from home. Across the front field. Across the highway. Through neighborhoods and across uninhabited outback. He was getting away from all that firework nonsense.

And the coyotes and I went back to being arch enemies on account of the chicken-stealing. Which is not the only stealing we fear at Ridgewood Farm.

We also fear baby stealing. But before we get to that, I would like to point out that it's never the chickens you *want* to get stolen that get stolen.

Stealing Chickens

Snickers. Photo by Lori Davis.

We got our first chickens from the farm supply. Every spring the farm supply stores get a few batches of cushballs to sell. I don't know how anyone passes them up. Cutest things in the world.

So, when you buy chicken cushballs at the farm supply, they are supposed to be sexed. Calm down. That's what you call it in chicken-buying circles.

Sexed chicken cushballs are chicks that are a day or two old, and some expert Asian has sorted them so you only get females. Again, with the judging. Look it up. The people who do this are Asian. Other people can't do it.

These Asians are about 90-95% accurate. That means, for every twenty baby chicks, you are likely to get one or two that turn into a rooster. We started with twenty chicks.

We got one or two that turned into roosters.

Now, we didn't know it at first. At first, they all looked the same, gender-wise. They grew, and as they did, different ones earned names for themselves. Zsa Zsa, for example, was a bit of a princess. She rose late and required special attention and treats.

Snickers had all the colors of a Snickers bar. And there was one that, despite being sold as a female, exhibited some very male characteristics. We took a page from old Saturday Night Live skits and named that one Pat.

Pat continued to grow non-female characteristics. And then, one day it happened. He put on a dance for the hens. One wing down, and quick feet. It was a classic James Brown move, which earned him the name James Brown.

James Brown, photo by Lori Davis. The dark spots on his comb are frostbite damage.

10% of our chicks turned out to be roosters. Snickers was the other one. But 100% of our roosters were mean. They chased people. They chased dogs. They chased guests at the guest house. They fought each other.

The worst thing they did was chase Lori's mom, who was nearly ninety. Snickers gave her a bruise on her leg, and it was time to act. I locked him in chicken time out, put him on bread and water, and left him for a week.

Snickers was a smart rooster. He never wanted that to happen again. So, I swear I'm not making this up, he never attacked anyone again except James Brown. He even chased James Brown away when he saw *him* chasing people.

James Brown was a different story. Correction didn't work for him. We started with gentle means, but graduated to kicking him away when he attacked, shoving him off with a walking stick, or chasing him around the yard till he was exhausted.

We tried endearing him to us. He got frostbite twice, both times requiring lengthy in-people-house stays with special treatment and food. He did special time inside when he ripped a spur off and was a bloody mess. He had rehab a few times when Snickers beat him up. Yet he still chased little kids and old people.

But when coyotes or foxes or owls or hawks or possums or raccoons or God only knows what else came, he made himself scarce. They never got *him*. We'd have been happy for him to be the victim. Happy might be strong. I never like to experience losing an animal.

Lori's mom, on the other hand, hated James Brown. If she could have figured voodoo out, she'd have been vengefully terrorizing him, torturing him with a rooster-shaped pin-cushion. If she had ever connected with that walking stick, he'd have been a goner.

But, James Brown died at a ripe, old, cranky age. Mean up to his last breath. He never got stolen by predators. But we still keet our guard up.

You never know when an ill-wind wafts up an unusual miscreant prone to thievery. Thievery of something we're more concerned about getting thove. I don't know why that isn't a word. It should be.

Stealing Children

Original Photo courtesy Pintrest user HSNSRCCK.
Artistic modifications by Barry Brown.

Every so often Lori gets a request from someone wanting to stay in the guest house that causes her a bit of alarm. She is more easily alarmed than I, but still, some were universally iffy. And hopefully unusual enough to satisfy the interest I piqued in you at the end of the last chapter.

One of the requests was clearly from a non-native English speaker. First of all, Lori doesn't allow huge parties. It says so right on the AirBnB site. Nice people often ask exactly what she means. "Hey, we were going to have our child from the college and a couple of her friends over. Is that okay?" Of course.

But when someone who doesn't speak English says they want to stay in the guest house to, "have a party with all their friends so they can sleep with them," and the message uses a couple of other vague references that could be euphemisms for Caligula-style orgies, she declines the request.

This one time, she got a message asking if she had a special rate for long-term stays. The person wanted to stay three months because he was coming from Brazil to America "to get a baby." Apparently, that takes three months. She just didn't respond, hoping like a noisy neighbor kid, this guy would eventually just go away.

He didn't.

The next message a couple of weeks later was, "Can I come by and check out the house because I'm in town." Her response to this message was to demand that I be around when this weirdo showed up in case he pulled some freaky stuff.

Well, it wasn't a weirdo after all, and he didn't pull any freaky stuff. It wasn't a pirate stealing babies to crew his dark, menacing vessel. It wasn't the boogey man. It wasn't the Pied Piper. Just a regular guy.

This regular guy was a Brazilian guy, an attorney in their military. A guy whose girl, thirty years before, had gotten pregnant with twins. Only she didn't have a good liver, and doctors decided they had to take one of the twins. Not terrible insurance-driven American doctors, but real doctors. And *they, the doctors, chose* which twin they were taking. Not the parents. I don't want to get bogged down in politics, but when we're talking about doctors deciding things about life or death like this, I am definitely pro-choice. Pro-patient-choice. I'm pro doctors-staying-in-their-lane-and-leaving-us-the-hell-alone choice.

Anyway, when she got ready to deliver the other baby, her liver crapped out, and both she and the baby died. Can this get any worse?

Well, along about age 50, this regular Brazilian guy hadn't found the right girl again. The right girl to wife up, and to have kids with. But he wanted a child.

The only countries that would let a single man have a surrogate baby — he said, fact checkers do yo thing, I couldn't care less — were the U.S.A., Russia, and Ukraine. Hindsight being 20/20, he's lucky he didn't pick Russia and/or the Ukraine. Some of his associates in the surrogate baby-getting world did, and they're having a devil of a time trying to get the moms and babies to safety.

I had no idea how many people it took to have a surrogate baby. I would have bet, and lost, that the answer was two. Same as any old baby. But it turns out that you have three: the sperm donor, the egg donor, and the womb donor. I guess that's for legal reasons. No one had more than one-third interest and couldn't screw the new parent(s) out of their agreed-upon kid.

This regular guy, I'll call him Otavio because that's a nice Brazilian name, had more bad luck. The first egg donor had eggs that didn't do so hot with his sperm. And the first womb donor went walkabout, leaving no forwarding info, except with her dealer presumably.

When we met Otavio, he was on try number two. The egg donor was some kind of model from South Africa. The womb donor was a nurse here in town. And that's why he was coming to get a baby here, you see. Because that's where the womb and baby were going to be.

Get ready to feel some sentiment. Otavio came for *every single* check-up that lady had with her OB/GYN team. That's why he was able to visit the house beforehand. He was in town for an ultrasound. In town from Brazil. The country. I'd wager few dads *in* country make it to all the OB/GYN appointments before their child is born.

When he came for the three-month stay, he had to travel from here to Houston to a Brazilian consulate for passport and citizenship junk for his baby.

He had to travel to Miami to engage the services of this special Brazilian "help you start off right with your newborn" expert gal. It's a specific career in Brazil with a Portuguese name and everything. At least, that's the best I could understand from talking with her in Spanish as I drove her back from the airport when she came to coach Otavio. No telling what she really said. My Spanish is better than people who don't speak Spanish, but only marginally.

He had to arrange stuff with the airline. And I don't even know who all. He held court here for various family members to come visit the new baby. It was wild.

And he had to complete his Brazilian manhood rites.

Boy, that sure sounds interesting doesn't it? Turns out it's a little more sentiment-meets-Wendell Berry than that. Otavio said there's a saying in Brazil that every man should write a book, raise a child, and plant a tree.

Otavio had written a book. Now he was raising a lovely little girl. All he lacked was planting a tree.

The city where Otavio lived in a small apartment in Brazil was not ideal for tree-planting. So, he decided to do it here.

He got a crabapple tree to plant for his new daughter. She was a little young to do it for herself at that point. The crabapple is one of the earliest blooming trees here. Great for pollinators.

He planted an oak for himself. Smack in the middle of a pasture where it can provide shade for livestock in the future.

He regularly sends us photos of that beautiful little girl as she grows and develops. We send photos of their two trees. We're getting the better deal out of this photo-swap.

And hopefully you'll agree with me that the start to our relationship with Otavio was atypical if not downright unusual.

Surprise, surprise, surprise

2024 Total eclipse photo from Ridgewood Farm.
Photo courtesy of James Gober.

Look, I've seen Apocalypto. An eclipse can be pretty darned unusual. It's so unusual, you might see it as reason enough to quit cutting out your neighbors' hearts and tossing their heads down the stairs. And we were slated to have one of the most unusual of modern times.

It was a surprise for me. I don't keep track of who's having an eclipse and when. I don't know what I'm having for dinner till a few minutes before I start digging in the fridge, usually.

Then my brother showed up wearing a tee-shirt advertising our grandparents' hometown. Advertising to come for the eclipse. In two years.

This nowhere town of about three thousand had extra housing and port-a-potties and activities and concerts already set up a couple of years in advance. In researching that, I found that we'd be on the "path of totality" here as well.

"Path of totality" is just one of the terms that got en vogue here as all the usual people became unusual eclipse experts for a season. If you're not into eclipses, the path of totality is this line along the earth where you can watch the complete, full, totally-blocked-sun eclipse. More on that later.

Because he'd alerted me to this with the tee-shirt, I asked my brother about it. He and his wife had watched a total eclipse on the West Coast a few years earlier.

They had driven about an hour to a prime campground viewing location. On the day of the eclipse, people swarmed in like flies on a gut-wagon. The authorities said there had been something like twenty million people who came over to see the thing. Despite your experience with my exaggerations in this book, I don't think that one is. How do you exaggerate twenty million, anyway? And our eclipse was predicted to provide twice the length of time in total eclipse (when the moon completely blocks out the sun) as the one out west.

He recommended I rent out little squares of pasture for tent camping or no-hook-up RV camping. People had done that in Oregon and northern California and made a mint, which nowadays would go nicely toward a semester of college or a tank of gas or something.

He said it was unbelievable the amount of trash that eclipse-viewers generated, spilling over every dumpster at every business all along their route home. The route home that was an hour drive going, but which took them half a day going back due to the post-eclipse traffic.

Here went the calculator. I had perfect access to escape highways, so no bottlenecks after it was over and viewers wanted to get back home. I had plenty of fields and no need to get rich quick, so I'd rent spots four times as large as the ones rented out west. I would be ready.

Ridgewood Farm Eclipse logo. Design by Barry Brown.

I secured porta-potties. I reserved a dumpster. We made a farm website. I lined up friends who catered to make some great meals available.

I figured very conservatively that we could provide a stellar experience to our guests and still make enough to put a guest cabin in the woods for a second AirBnB offering.

Reservations and inquiries began pouring in at the rate of one. Not one per day or hour or anything, just one. One hippy-sounding fella asking if the town planned to "go dark." Second eclipse chaser term.

"Going dark" is when a town respects the eclipse opportunity so much that they ensure all the street lights and night lights and parking lot lights and other light pollution normally gunking up urban night skies all get turned off.

Searcy was very serious about *looking* serious about the eclipse. They learned that there would be one, that we would be in the zone of totality, and for some of the longest times. They learned that about six months before it happened.

They quickly found someone with a resume unrelated to eclipses, crowds, preparations, or any other similar thing, and hired her to be the eclipse organizer.

I went to the first meeting.

She had no idea what "going dark" meant. Once I told her, she said that would be too hard to do. There went the interest of the serious eclipse chasers.

She was good at printing flyers. Her flyers seriously said, "LOTS OF FUN

ACTIVITIES!" with no specifics listed. "LIVE MUSIC!" with no band name given because all the bands in the US and Canada were already booked by other towns that had been on the ball with their planning.

Well, it sounds like I'm venting. You are free to call it that. I would have liked to build another option for your staying pleasure at Ridgewood Farm. And now I'll have to find another funding source.

Because we had no eclipse guests.

Not entirely true. The AirBnB was rented. It was rented as far out as AirBnB lets guests book, which is another thing you can look up if you're interested.

Now, that was an unusual couple. You will never in a million years guess what he did for a living unless you cheat and look ahead. He was an aeronautical engineer!

Wait, huh? You say that's not unusual? You with all this judgment in your heart. He designed and sold competition-grade rubber band aircraft. Look who's saucy now. I bet THAT is so unusual you didn't even know there WERE competition-grade rubber band aircraft.

Yep. Turns out they have competitions at all academic levels and junior Olympics and everything. Probably

would have been an original Olympic sport

if the Greeks had invented rubber bands.

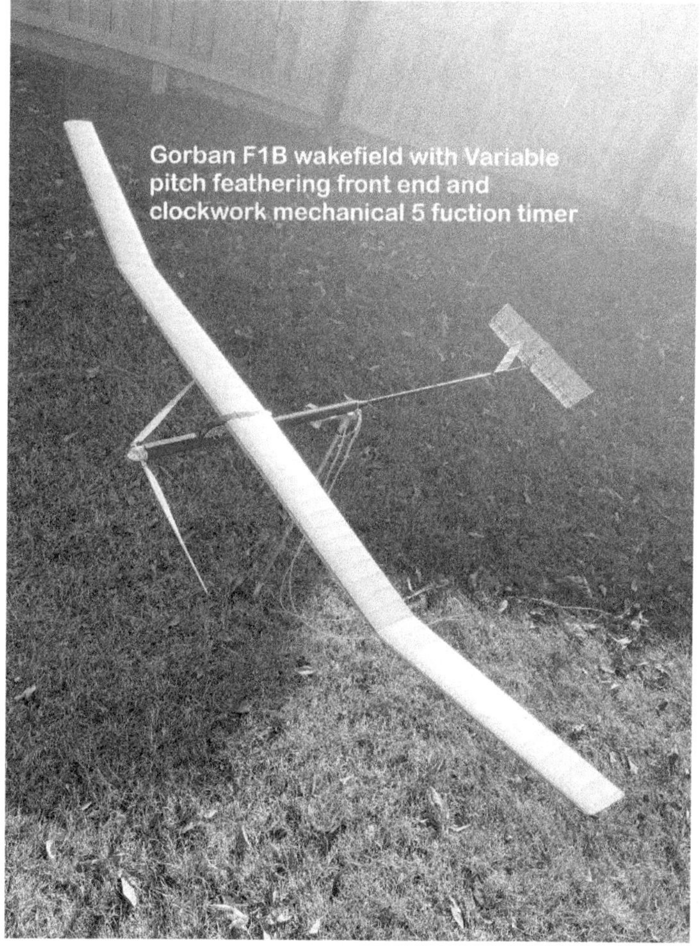

*Photo courtesy Hummingbird Model Products. Artistically
modified by Barry Brown. This site sold USED rubber band
planes like this STARTING at $450. And they were sold out.*

This guy said well-designed rubber band planes go for ... well, I don't remember the distance, but the way you've been so far, you wouldn't believe me anyway. I do remember that some would fly circles in a school gym and stay aloft for longer than Noah was on the ark. Or something like that.

This man and his wife were real eclipse chasers. They knew about our eclipse when they were in the third grade or thereabouts. They booked the AirBnB as far out as possible.

He showed me photos of previous ones they'd seen. Check THIS out. the ground makes a cool photo! All the gaps in the leaves of the trees, through the magic of optics and physics and so on, they put the image of the eclipse on the ground! So

Crescent shapes on the ground. Photo by Barry Brown.

pre-full eclipse, when you still can't look at the sun, watch the light spots on the ground. They'll get long and skinny, then crescent-shaped like the sun allegedly is right then. But they won't melt your eyeballs looking at them like the sun will. That's how they filmed that scene in Indiana Jones, anyone will tell you.

Well, I knew what an eclipse was. But I didn't know how cool it was. There was no looking at it early. That sun is no joke.

Then all of a sudden, it got cooler and darker. Then animals got chill and some lay down. Things got quiet.

You still couldn't look at the sun at all until the full eclipse. It was still paint-peeling bright. But then, when the fullness fulled or whatever we call it, you could look up there and see that black circle and that ring of fire, and it was awe-inspiring.

And it'll come here again! 2045 or 2048 or something. I can't remember which. I might be here. Or I might not. I don't know if Airbnb will let you book that far in advance.

But if they do ...

Book Your Stay at Ridgewood Farm Today!

Now you've read the history and the stories, real and imagined. Come relax and enjoy the peace. Toss the chickens some scratch. Milk a goat. Hand-feed treats to the cows. Saunter down by the pond or through the fields.

You'll enjoy gobbling up Lori's scones. You can cook up a mess of farm-fresh, absolutely free-range eggs.

Come live the life you've read about, if only for a few days. We would love you to be a new Ridgewood Farm friend.

And to take us full circle, you can sit.
You can breathe it in. You can rest and
enjoy the old soul that is Ridgewood Farm.

*(Click the link to find the Farmhouse at
Ridgewood Farm on Airbnb's website.)*

A Note About Indie Publishing

Word-of-mouth is crucial for any author to succeed. Especially Indie-Published authors. If you enjoyed *My Ridgewood Farm Experiences*, please leave a review online—anywhere you are able, Amazon, Goodreads, Bookbug. Even if it's just a sentence or two. Post a BookTok video. Everything helps.

I cannot express how much I sincerely appreciate you doing that. It will help me enormously, and I'll do my best to bring you more stories you love!

Thanks!

Barry Brown

Also by This Author:

NO MORE KINGS?? From what I've read, **NOT THIS KING** would sum up the movement better. Because it's all about this one versus that one. This party versus that. But I'm a REAL No More Kings kind of guy. And for me it started a couple of decades ago. This book is that journey. Do we have something better than monarchy or not?

Animal Zoo is written at a middle grade level. But the concepts are applicable at all ages. On the surface, it is a story about a group of young animals living in a zoo founded on the ideals of fairness and equality. The zoo founders wanted to create a better society than the one they left behind under the rule of the lion king. As the young animals grow up, they begin to question whether the zoo lives up to its promises.

Did you like George Orwell's **Animal Farm?** You'll love **Animal Zoo!**

Animal Zoo is a must-read for anyone interested in examining American Society. This thought-provoking story sparks conversations about class divisions, corruption, media influence, and injustice.

Coming Soon!

In time for Christmas, release in Smmer/Fall 2026!

You know the story of Rudolph, but how did Santa Claus come to have Dasher, or Dancer, or Prancer, or Vixen? Not to mention Comet or Cupid, much less Donner or Blitzen. You have no idea, because the legend has never been recorded since the dawn of time! UNTIL NOW that is! The entire story of Santa, the elves, Missus Claus, and the eight reindeer besides Rudolph, written and illustrated by Orso Marrone in the chow hall at the military prison at Fort Leavenworth.

Who is God? Is He just a powerful bean-counting bookkeeper in the sky?

Who are you? Is who you are more important than what you do?

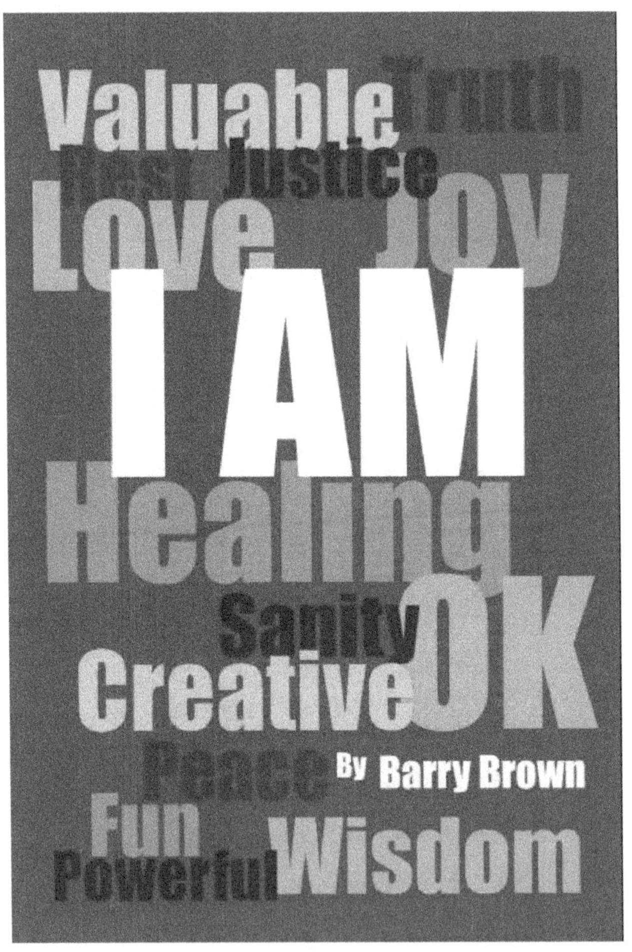

Is there more to Heaven than cloud-sitting and harp twonking?

What is repentance? Grace? Forgiveness?
Does Orthodox Christianity give the best
answers to these questions, or do they come
from somewhere else?

If you've ever struggled with any of these
questions, this is the book for you! I AM
confident you'll be more comfortable, more full
of God's peace with your answers after reading
I AM.

https://barrybrown.art/books/i-am/01d785ab-69a2-4f70-9c9e-f453051b4cac

Award-winning short stories by Barry Brown. Many genres, many lengths. Westerns, romance, sci-fi, memoir, flash fiction, holiday stories, fantasy, and stories defying categorization.

The only thing tying these stories together is judges loved them all! Well, that and they were written by the same guy.

www.ingramcontent.com/pod-product-compliance
Lightning Source LLC
Chambersburg PA
CBHW070822110726
47973CB00028B/275/J